NO JOURNEY WILL BE TOO LONG

FRIENDSHIP IN CHRISTIAN LIFE

José Tolentino Mendonça

Paulist Press
New York / Mahwah, NJ

Unless noted otherwise, the Scripture quotations contained herein are from the New Revised Standard Version: Catholic Edition, Copyright © 1989 and 1993, by the Division of Christian Education of the National Council of the Churches of Christ in the United States of America. Used by permission. All rights reserved.

Cover image by Anna Omelchenko / Shutterstock.com
Cover and book design by Lynn Else

Originally published in Portugal as *Nenhum Caminho será Longo: Para uma Teologia da Amizade.*

Copyright © 2012, INSTITUTO MISSIONÁRIO FILHAS DE SÃO PAULO— PAULINAS EDITORA Rua Francisco Salgado Zenha, 11—2685-332 Prior Velho—Portugal www.paulinas.pt.

English translation by Mary John Ronayne, OP, © 2013, Paulinas Editora.

All rights reserved. No part of this publication may be reproduced, stored in a retrieval system, or transmitted in any form or by any means, electronic, mechanical, photocopying, recording, scanning, or otherwise, without the prior written permission of the Publisher. Requests to the Publisher for permission should be addressed to the Permissions Department, Paulist Press, 997 Macarthur Boulevard, Mahwah, NJ 07430, (201) 825-7300, fax (201) 825-8345, or online at www.paulistpress.com.

Library of Congress Cataloging-in-Publication Data
Mendonça, José Tolentino.
    [Nenhum caminho será longo. English]
    No journey will be too long : friendship in Christian life / José Tolentino Mendonça.
        pages cm
    Original Portuguese title: Nenhum caminho será longo : para uma teologia da amizade.
    ISBN 978-0-8091-4897-4 (pbk. : alk. paper) — ISBN 978-1-58768-420-3 (ebook)
    1. Friendship—Religious aspects—Christianity. 2. Spirituality—Christianity. I. Title.
    BV4647.F7M4613 2014
    241`.6762—dc23
                                                            2014022350

ISBN 978-0-8091-4897-4 (paperback)
ISBN 978-1-58768-420-3 (e-book)

Published in the United States in 2015 by Paulist Press
997 Macarthur Boulevard
Mahwah, New Jersey 07430

www.paulistpress.com

Printed and bound in the
United States of America

CONTENTS

iii

*"With your friend beside you,
no journey will be too long"*

Japanese proverb

FOREWORD

This book by José Tolentino Mendonça combines a profound sense of the richness of friendship with its discretion, its quiet acceptance of limits. Such an understanding of our relationship with God balances the more erotic and conjugal metaphors that have dominated recent spirituality, and brings to light the gentle respectfulness of God's love for us, which lifts us up into the equality of the Triune love. This theme is explored with a rare range of reference, a deep immersion in the Word of God, this word of friendship that never ceases to summon us on the way, but also a rich understanding of the classical roots of our own civilization, a sensitivity to poetry too often lacking in theology, and the insights that can be welcomed from other cultures. It is a deeply civilized book, to be savored.

Timothy Radcliffe, OP

PREFACE

It would seem that in our day we only know how to talk about love. At the same time, the steady inflation in the use of the word itself is accompanied, obviously, by a diminution in its expressive force, as if it had been taken over by equivocation and a kind of sleepwalking. The more we talk about love, the less we know what we are talking about. But this does not stop us doing it! We use the same word in speaking of conjugal love and our membership to a sports club, our relationship with our parents and the things we eat, the deepest, as well as the most trivial, ambitions. Everything is love.

In the field of religion, the situation is unfortunately not very different. The word *love* is so overused that it militates against realism and the deepening of the ways of faith. References to love abound in homilies, catechetical discourses, moral propositions: forming a dizzy pathway that serves to attenuate if not actually neutralize its meaning. We have grown accustomed to hearing appeals for love, and we receive them or repeat them without much in the way of discernment. I am convinced that an important part of the problem is a lack of reflection on friendship. We speak ambiguously in terms of love when discussing affective relationships and practices/customs that would be much more meaningful if we were to think of them as forms of friendship. And this also in terms of the relationship of believers with God!

My hope is that this book will help us to think about the meaning and relevance of friendship in various situations: in our personal lives, in the context of communities and believers, in social relationships. Friendship is a universal experience and represents for each individual an irreplaceable process of humanization and hope. Nevertheless, we also need wisdom, including a spiritual wisdom, which will enable us to live it more fully.

"Our friends are part of our life," wrote Raïssa Maritain. But there is more to it than that: they widen our lives, helping to make them more luminous and authentic; they offer us lightness and depth; they purify it with the truth, leaven it with humor, and insist that it is made for the future. Friends bear witness to our heart that there is always a journey to be undertaken and that no journey will be too long.

1

AND IF WE WERE TO SPEAK OF FRIENDSHIP INSTEAD OF LOVE?

In the Bible, we find a number of images of deep affection that are used to describe our relationship with God. They correspond to two basic paradigms, one of which is the well-established image of love. In fact, the Bible describes God on the basis of the experience of conjugal or, we might say, erotic love. Very often, the relationship between God and his people is expressed in terms of a bridal relationship, a wedding feast, with the emphasis on complete union, an intermediate state between joyous union and possession. This state is longingly evoked in the Book of Jeremiah: "I remember the devotion of your youth, your love as a bride, how you followed me in the wilderness, in a land not sown" (2:2). God yearns for this intimacy, for the time when the hearts of his people had not gone astray but had been centered exclusively on dialogue with him. We might say that it was an exclusive relationship. There was no other face on earth, for beyond this face there was only the desert. Or again, in chapter 16 of the Book of Ezekiel: "I passed by you…"—God is speaking of his people—

> and looked on you; you were at the age for love. I spread the edge of my cloak over you, and covered your nakedness: I pledged myself to you and entered into a covenant with you, says the Lord GOD, and you became mine. Then I bathed you

1

with water and washed off the blood from you, and anointed you with oil. I clothed you with embroidered cloth and with sandals of fine leather; I bound you in fine linen and covered you with rich fabric. I adorned you with ornaments: I put bracelets on your arms, a chain on your neck, a ring on your nose, earrings in your ears, and a beautiful crown upon your head. You were adorned with gold and silver, while your clothing was of fine linen, rich fabric, and embroidered cloth. You had choice flour and honey and oil for food. You grew exceedingly beautiful, fit to be a queen. (16:8–13)

From the literary point of view, this magnificent text presents Israel as a bride richly adorned for a definitive bridal encounter. Apart from the Song of Songs, the book in which this bridal image is taken furthest is perhaps the one attributed to the prophet Hosea. In it, the people of God is described as a woman who has betrayed her husband but, in spite of this, her husband continues to reach out to her with bonds of love and to be faithful to her. God's longing comes to us through the mouth of the prophet: "On that day, says the LORD, you will call me, 'My husband,' and no longer will you call me, 'My Baal.'...And I will take you for my wife for ever'" (Hos 2:16, 19).

These are brief examples of a vast theological heritage, and they reveal how widespread is this custom of using metaphors to describe love, with the clear intention of establishing a radical link between God and the believer. Clearly, the paradigm of love continues, and will continue, to be both valid and inspiring. Nevertheless, where our relationship with God is concerned, it remains no more than one possible image, an attempt at approximation, a stammered expression of this great mystery. Hence, it must not be taken to be the only way of expressing it. The Bible insists pedagogically on a plurality of approaches, some of which are centered on a paradigm that we will reflect on here and which needs to be rediscovered, namely friendship.

THE DIFFERENCE BETWEEN LOVE AND FRIENDSHIP

In defining our spiritual journey, it is important to recognize the difference between love and friendship. We find it very easy, not to say almost automatic, to use the vocabulary of love, which could easily turn into the grammar of a sleepwalker. We say "I love" even when this does not imply any deep feeling or represent a commitment of any kind. It is important to reflect on what we are saying when we say that we love God. From this point of view, the model of friendship can help us to perceive, in contrast to the sleepwalking tendency of our statements, what is and what can be our relationship with God. The danger inherent in the language of love is to lose oneself in indefiniteness, to plunge into the boundlessness of subjectivity: we do not quite know what love is; it is always everything; it is a colossal task; and far too often this undistinguishable totality of love ends up in a disillusioned rhetorical vacuum. Friendship is a more objective form, more concretely conceived, and possibly easier to live.

According to Françoise Dolto, friendship is something that is very interesting, because in friendship there is safety without pressure. We are quite content to remain ignorant of anything that we do not know about the other. The fact that we do not know everything about the other does not affect our relationship with him or her, and this is something that love finds it difficult to accept. In love, the revelation must be total and single: single in frankness, in openness, in knowledge without reservation or concealment of any kind. In friendship we are better able to accept difference, a certain distance that is not seen as a barrier to trust. On the contrary, it is a condition for the revelation of oneself. This distance makes people

3

free to be authentic; it frees friends from any temptation to dominate. Friendship does not have that need to possess that is often characteristic of an unduly egoistic, exaggeratedly narcissistic love. Even more so than in a love relationship, the relationship between friends is fertilized by the acceptance of anticipated limits. Possibly, the great difference between love and friendship lies in the fact that love reaches always for the unbounded, and is always suspicious of restrictions and frontiers. If, in a love relationship, you hide something from me, sooner or later this will come to be an unbearable weight whereas, in the case of a friendship, we cope quite happily with constrictions, we accept that the other has a life that does not include us and goes beyond us. It is not that in love too there has to be acceptance of all this, but this is not its idiom, its specificity. The friend is the one who is part of our life without ceasing to be another.

IN PRAISE OF FRIENDSHIP IN THE CONSTRUCTION OF A ROAD FOR THE BELIEVER

In fact, it would be important for us to establish our relationship with God in terms of friendship. Friendship can constitute a creative model for a believer's way forward even if we continue to talk in terms of love. But understanding this relationship exclusively on the basis of the love model frequently leads to anxiety, an inability to act, and a lack of incentive. Since the predominating element in love is that of the "all or nothing" that is beyond us, we end up in the nothing side of things, eaten up with feelings of guilt, and endeavoring to put the picture back together with patches of ritualism. We idealize our relationship with God to such an extent that we find it very difficult to accept that it does not fit into what, for us, are not only perfect examples but the only ones that would satisfy us. We complain about not having the faith of St. Teresa of

Avila or John Paul II; that we are not as prayerful as our mother's mother, or do not possess the deep commitment that we envy in our neighbor. At the same time, this provides us with an excuse for not doing the only thing that God is really looking for from us: to be ourselves. We fail to realize that authentic faith is always a faith made of crumbs, as we learn from the story of the Canaanite woman:

> Jesus left that place and went away to the district of Tyre and Sidon. Just then a Canaanite woman from that region came out and started shouting, "Have mercy on me, Lord, Son of David; my daughter is tormented by a demon." But he did not answer her at all. And his disciples came and urged him, saying, "Send her away, for she keeps shouting after us." He answered, "I was sent only to the lost sheep of the house of Israel." But she came and knelt before him, saying, "Lord, help me." He answered, "It is not fair to take the children's food and throw it to the dogs." She said, "Yes, Lord, yet even the dogs eat the crumbs that fall from their masters' table." Then Jesus answered her, "Woman, great is your faith! Let it be done for you as you wish." And her daughter was healed instantly. (Matt 15:21–28)

It is extremely important to embrace the nothings as fragments of the truth, as parts of an intimacy that can be experienced but not possessed; that one can listen to deeply but not cling to. The relationship to be built up with God is always in freedom, allowing God to be God and recognizing that God allows me to be myself. God does not treat me like a puppet. What expectations has God for me? What does he hope for from me? What do I think God is hoping for from me? At times, we drown in a confused conception of all this, and we heap blame upon blame upon ourselves in a painful interior imprisonment. We expect punishments that God in his infinite mercy

(Eph 2:4) does not wish to inflict on us. We project onto God expectations that he cannot have concerning us because he respects our freedom, he accepts the unknown there is in us, the stranger living within us, the enigma that we are.

GOD KNOCKS AT OUR DOOR BUT DOES NOT BREAK IT DOWN

God comes in the cool of the evening to visit the garden occupied by the first human couple, but Adam and Eve hide from God. And God asks, "Where are you?" (Gen 3:9). In a combination of hermeneutics and humor, the Rabbinic tradition says that this is possibly the only superfluous phrase in the Bible. How is it possible for God to ask, "Where are you?" If God knows everything, this is a completely artificial question. But if he does not know where the first human couple is, then God's omniscience is called into question. It is an embarrassing moment in the biblical revelation. The rabbis, however, extract a rich spiritual interpretation from it. Only we ourselves can say where we are, they tell us. God does not pursue us, but in a friendly way waits for us to tell him where we are.

What a change there would be if we were to take this seriously! God respects our freedom and his expectation in our regard is not that of a possessive partner, of a rival who does not let us have space in which to breathe and be creative. Our relationship with God is not a cage, but an opening out to an ever-wider space. God waits for everyone. And he waits with patience. "Listen! I am standing at the door, knocking; if you hear my voice and open the door, I will come in to you and eat with you, and you with me" (Rev 3:20).

At times like this, I often find myself thinking of Edith Södergran's poem, as a prayer to be learned in silence.

There is no-one in the world except God who has time for me

which is why the flowers walk for Him
and the last of the ants.
The forget-me-not asks for a brighter shine
in her blue eyes
and the ant asks for greater strength
for carrying the piece of straw,
and the bees ask him for a more triumphal song
among the purple roses.

And God is present in everything.
Without hoping to, the old lady found her cat by
    the well
and the cat her mistress.
Great was the delight of both
and greater still when God left them together
and wished for them this marvelous friendship
which lasted fourteen years.

God's expectation is that, in the independence and
uniqueness that we are, we can live a beautiful life, risk living
an authentic life. He is not the metaphysical spy who is ready
to keep a record of our faults or misdeeds or else to reward us
for our good actions and piety. As St. Irenaeus wrote as early
as the second century: "The One who cannot be grasped, comprehended or seen, allows himself to be seen, comprehended
and grasped by men, that he may give life to those who see
him and receive him….The glory of God is man fully alive."
God's expectation is that each one of us should be himself or
herself and live, live, live. This is, in fact, the experience of
friendship.

FRIENDSHIP IS A PASSING BY...

We need to purify the images of God that are spelled out
with our feelings of insecurity and fear. The paradigm of
friendship applied to our relationship with God can produce

an extraordinarily liberating result. Friendship is the positive acceptance of limitation. There comes a moment when you are going home to your house and I am going to mine and this is completely undramatic. On the contrary, we know that we shall be meeting again and that even when we do not see each other, we are not losing sight of each other; that the essential remains intact even at a distance. To view our relationship with God in these terms fills us with peace and joy; there is an inner breath that helps us; our prayer begins to breathe in a way that comes partly from ourselves instead of placing us on a plane of pure abstraction. For, unfortunately, most of our prayer possesses neither body nor soul, it has no blood or truth, it contains neither clay nor spirit. Deep down, we persist in retaining an image of God that calls on us for sacrifices when the God of Jesus Christ is looking for a good life, a life lived to the full, a life raised to his joy.

Moses constitutes an example of faith based on friendship. Moses spoke to God face to face, as a man speaks to his friend (Exod 33:11). We need this too, to feel that we are in God's presence and speaking with him as a man or a woman speaks with a friend, whether male or female. We need to reach this fluidity of relationship and feel that there is an eye-to-eye, heart-to-heart relationship. This kind of closeness does not impinge on God's transcendence. God continues to say: "Moses, I will make all my goodness pass before you. I will show you my glory, but you cannot see my face. You shall see my back, but my face shall not be seen" (see Exod 33:17–23). This is what friends experience. On the one hand, they look into each other's eyes, but on the other, they are willing to see only a part of the whole, in the incomplete vision, the unfinished gesture. In friendship, we accept from the other what he or she gives us or can give, and we make of this a joyful point of departure. The desire to know everything, to rip open, to scrutinize, is the projection of a desire to dominate; it is a wish for power.

Friendship is a passing-by. God allows his beauty to pass before Moses and Moses sees part of it, the part that he can see. If we were to live our spiritual experience like this, it would be much more peaceful, much more adult, and certainly much more fruitful. We have to open wide our hands, and let God pass by. Easter faith is quite simply this: a passing over, a moving across, a beauty parade, epiphany, revelation that one cannot touch. *Noli me tangere*—"Do not touch me" (John 20:17), said the risen Lord to Mary. We are in God's presence as friends, in the gratuitousness of a relationship.

LOVING GOD FOR NOTHING

God respects our freedom; he does not seek to capture us. God the Creator loves our ability to create. We are not static works in his hands. It is true that we are always being overcome by the temptation to a certain providentialism ("God help me, God do this, do that"), when the really important thing is the experience of knowing that God is, and that we are his friends. God does this without wishing to control us, to domesticate us, without invading our secret space. There are times when the yearning we have to be spared the sufferings of the present moment turns religion into something very comfortable, made to our own measure, as if religion were a club of escapists. If religion is a kind of life insurance, let's go in for it, why not? However, the journey of friendship is quite different. It is necessary to love God for nothing. To love him, and that's all! Angelus Silesius wrote: "The rose is without why; it blooms because it blooms; it cares not for itself; asks not if it's seen." Or, as Gertrude Stein wrote: "Rose is a rose is a rose is a rose."

To love God for nothing. St. Thérèse of the Child Jesus used to say: "Even if there were no heaven, I would still love God." We have to get beyond a particular conception of Christianity as being a machine churning out punishments and rewards. The saints teach us the mystery of divine friendship: accept whatever God wishes to give me, accept the night and the nothing, the silence and the delay, accept the grace and the weakness. Accept, accept. Make of everything a journey. When we prepare ourselves for this, we are at last entering into an experience of friendship. We do not appreciate our friends merely for what they give us: they can come with empty hands and we love them just the same. Truth to tell, there are times when things, in friendship, only confuse matters. Our relationship with God, too, passes through empty hands, where the essential is the encounter, that which mysteriously and gratuitously passes from heart to heart.

THERE IS NO NEED FOR WORDS

What tells us that two people whom we do not know are friends? By the way they talk to each other? Yes, of course. By the way they laugh? Again, yes, of course. But even more so by the fact that they clearly embrace each other's silence with serenity and joy. Friends can be together in silence. In the case of acquaintances, silence is an embarrassment; we immediately feel the need to start a conversation, to fill the empty space with communication: to remain silent makes us uncomfortable. Silence is never a matter of embarrassment between friends. The silence is a bond that unites. Let us look at a text by the Brazilian theologian, Ruben Alves:

A friend is the person in whose company it is not necessary to talk. This is how to discover how many friends you have: if the silence between you and another makes you uncomfortable, if, when there is a silence, you try to find words to fill the empty space and keep the conversation going, then the person you are with is not a friend, because a friend is someone whom we seek out, not for whatever we might be going to do together….The difference lies in the fact that when the person we are with is not a real friend, once our cheerful and animated programme comes to an end it is followed by a silence and an emptiness which are unbearable. At this

10

moment, the other becomes a nuisance who is taking up space and whose departure one longs for. We want to get rid of that person. With a friend, things are different; there is no need for words.

I think a notice stating "There is no need for words" should be placed in church entrances. To turn prayer into a kind of endless chatter is a useless waste of time. But if we accept that friendship is being together even without speaking, then the practice of prayer becomes deeper, touches new levels, opens us to other dimensions of being. There is no need for words. All that is needed is the consolation of being together. A friend is someone whose very presence brings joy, apart altogether from anything that is said or done. Friendship is not a hostage to programs just as prayer begs not to be taken over by speech. "When you are praying, do not heap up empty phrases" (Matt 6:7), urges Jesus.

THE POETICS OF FRIENDSHIP

A story from the East tells of a solitary tree that was visible at the top of a mountain. It had not always been so. In the past, the mountain had been covered with magnificent trees, tall and slender, which the woodcutters had felled and sold one by one. But that one tree was crooked and so could not be transformed into planks. Being useless for the woodcutters' purposes, they left it where it was. Later, there came men trading in essences in search of perfumed woods, but as the crooked tree had no perfume, it was rejected and, once again, left where it was. It survived because it was useless. Today it is alone at the top of the mountain, it is visible from a long way off and travelers long to sit under its shade.

A friend is like that tree that lives because it is of no use. Our spirituality, too, needs to be useless, in order to survive for more than a moment, to be more than needed for a particular reason, to survive, to welcome the eternal dance. It can often happen that a particular need poisons our relationship with God. Now, a friend is not needed: he or she is the chosen one, the gratuitous one. We are right to say: "A friend is a brother or sister I have chosen." I choose, I feel I have been chosen: an exchange of unexplained gratuitousness.

A friend is like that tree. It can even be useful, but it is not its usefulness that makes it a friend. Its useless and faithful presence in our lives makes our solitude an experience of communion. In the presence of a friend, we know that we are not alone. We read this in the unforgettable passage in the Prophet Isaiah: "Do not fear, for I have redeemed you; I have called you by name, you are mine. When you pass through the waters, I will be with you; and through the rivers, they shall not overwhelm you; when you walk through fire you shall not be burned, and the flame shall not consume you....Do not fear, for I am with you" (Isa 43:1–2, 5).

So let us think of our relationship with God as being a relationship of friendship. Let us reflect on how illuminating the experience of freedom can be in the structuring of our relationship with God: our acceptance of the other; the serene acknowledgment of limits: differentiation, the lack of domination, freedom, gratuitousness, pure contemplation, not holding back, the perception that the other is passing through my life, and that this passing through bears fruit within me. Friends are interested in the concrete, in the detail, in the small scale, in the simple story, in the seemingly useless, in the undisturbed passage of time, in the froth on the daydream. To use a lovely expression of Walter Benjamin's, friends know that each second that passes is a tiny door through which the Messiah may enter.

2

SOME BIBLICAL FRIENDSHIPS

The Bible recognizes the importance of true friendship and is not sparing in words designed to highlight its importance. The Book of Deuteronomy speaks of the friend (*réa*, in Hebrew) as the person "who is as your own soul" (13:6, ESV), and the Book of Proverbs says, "A true friend sticks closer than one's nearest kin" (18:24). In friendship, heart speaks to heart (see Prov 27:19) and as "perfume and incense make the heart glad, so friendship's sweetness comforts the soul" (Prov 27:9; alt. translation). In the Book of Sirach, we have praise of a true friend: "Faithful friends are a sturdy shelter; whoever finds one has found a treasure. Faithful friends are beyond price; no amount can balance their worth. Faithful friends are lifesaving medicine; and those who fear the Lord will find them" (6:14–16). However, anyone who wishes to understand more deeply the biblical conception of friendship needs to reflect on the stories that it contains. Here, too, the theology contained in the Bible is predominantly narrative. And let there be no doubt about it: we need this wisdom. The stories convey knowledge to us not by a process of abstraction, but with the intensity of an experience that we, too, are called upon to share.

GOD AND ABRAHAM

Our journey through the histories of friendship in the Bible takes us to this surprising reference that we find in the

Book of the Prophet Isaiah: "But you, Israel, my servant, Jacob whom I have chosen, the offspring of Abraham, my friend" (41:8). Here we have a list of different forms of relationship (servant, chosen one, friend), each one accompanied by the note of affection conveyed by the possessive adjective *my*. Behind each expression, there is a perception of what we are and what God is, since the statement is placed in the mouth of God. Now, together with the fundamental categories of "servant " and "chosen one" (which come from the field of the representation of power, in a type of arrangement closely allied to that which would later develop between lord and vassal), we have here a quite different category, that of "friend." How does Abraham become a "friend" of God? By building up a relationship of confidence (from which, more-over, the word *faith* is derived)? By means of a mutual covenant established between them? Undoubtedly. But also thanks to a series of minor details, daily, almost indescribable, occurrences that open up for us the characteristic universe of the grammar of friendship when we find:

> both looking in the same direction (Gen 15:5);
> both showing a concern expressed in gestures (Gen 15:1): [God said:] "Do not be afraid, Abram, I am your shield";
> both being involved in the practice of hospitality (Gen 18:1–5): "The LORD appeared to Abraham by the oaks of Mamre, as he sat at the entrance of his tent in the heat of the day. He looked up and saw three men standing near him. When he saw them, he ran from the tent entrance to meet them, and bowed down to the ground. He said, 'My lord, if I find favor with you, do not pass by your servant. Let a little water be brought, and wash your feet, and rest yourselves under the tree. Let me bring a little bread that you may refresh yourselves, and after that you may pass on.'"

GOD AND MOSES

Friendship with God is an open possibility. It is very important to note how it repeats itself. "When Moses entered the tent, the pillar of cloud would descend and stand at the entrance of the tent, and the LORD would speak with Moses....Thus the LORD used to speak to Moses face to face, as one speaks to a friend" (Exod 33:9, 11). In fact, God's revelation is not only the law, which can be inscribed on tablets of stone and there remain recorded for posterity; it is also written in the heart, as a living thing, a yearning that fills us, a mutual acceptance, an intimacy. Before it becomes normative, the experience of God is a mystical experience. And the norm must express and underlie this primary experience that is friendship, expressed as a covenant and in the timelessness of the "face to face, as one speaks to a friend."

RUTH AND NAOMI

Following the deaths of the two sons with whom she had lived, the widow Naomi said farewell to her two daughters-in-law, Orpah and Ruth, and prepared to return alone to the land of Israel. "I went away full, but the LORD has brought me back empty," she said in her distress (see Ruth 1:21). In a world full of repeated waves of migration, we continue to hear Naomi's lament every day. Emigrants leave home full of hope in a future that will redeem them but things do not always turn out like that. Very often, they are obliged to return to their point of departure poorer and in greater distress than before. Naomi had intended to depart alone, but Ruth insisted on sharing her fate. The promise of friendship that Ruth makes at this point to Naomi is one of the most memorable passages in the Bible: "Where you go, I will go; where you lodge, I will lodge; your people shall be my people, and your God my God. Where you die, I will die—there will I be buried. May the LORD do thus and so to me, and more as well, if even death parts me from you" (1:16–17). Naomi displays an equivalent concern for Ruth, and once they are in Israel, she devises a romantic stratagem to enable Ruth to meet another suitor and marry for a second time. When Naomi's plan bears fruit, Ruth, the foreigner, becomes part of the royal genealogy by becoming David's great-grandmother.

DAVID AND JONATHAN

An interesting element about this friendship, and one that is typical of its grammar, is that it was not, strictly speaking, sought out. It was a question of an immediate understanding occurring between two souls when they meet. Significantly, the Hebrew text of 1 Samuel 18:1 uses a passive form of the verb: "The soul of Jonathan was bound to the soul of David." In fact, friendship is a gift for which there is no explanation. That said, it is equally true that the way in which the friendship between them developed historically continues to be relevant. David had just defeated Goliath in a contest that revealed daring but also trust in God's protection. What David had done gave Jonathan an opportunity to come to know something about him. And there developed in Jonathan a feeling of admiration for David. At this point, it is perhaps relevant to cite the comment made by Aelred of Rievaulx, who saw in the spontaneous friendship between Jonathan and David a reflection illuminated by reason. The friendship was born "in the light of virtue": "Jonathan, the friend of virtue, was led to experience affection for a virtuous youth." On the other hand, the first Book of Samuel tells us that "Jonathan loved [David] as his own soul." This "as" implies both a recognition and an acceptance of equality. David was already a hero, but he was still no more than a shepherd, whereas Jonathan was the king's son. They would need to establish a relationship of equality between them in order to consider themselves friends. But the fact that Jonathan loves David as himself is also a reference to the fulfillment of the commandment "You shall love your neighbor as yourself" (Lev 19:18). Friendship is the fullness of the Law, indeed its perfection. When King Saul's feeling of insecurity and his pathology were manifested in a desire to persecute David, Jonathan was to come to the defense of his friend. At first he tried to effect a reconciliation with the king, but later protected David in secret. David and Jonathan deepened their friendship by means of a pact, which is a kind of sacrament. They said: "As for the matter about which you and I have spoken, the LORD is witness between you and me forever" (1 Sam 20:23). Friendship is an experience to which God himself bears witness. The friend makes it certain that God does not abandon us. The friendship of Jonathan and David was destined to become a model in both life and death. Faced with the implacable hatred of King Saul, the friends are forced to separate. It is a deeply felt parting, in which their emotions are clearly visible. And, scandalously for the culture of the time, the biblical text portrays two men in tears who embrace: "David emerged from his hiding place and fell on his face to the ground, and bowed three times; and they kissed one another, and wept with one another, until David recovered himself" (RSV), but David was more deeply moved than his friend. "Then Jonathan said to David, 'Go in peace, since both of us have sworn in the name of the LORD, saying, 'The LORD shall be between me and you, and between my descendants and your descendants for ever'" (1 Sam 20:41–42). In fact, this pact of friendship was to persist beyond death. When Jonathan died at the hands of the Philistines, David dedicated to him one of the loveliest elegies of all poetry, which is in itself an encomium of friendship.

> I am distressed for you, my brother Jonathan;
> greatly beloved were you to me;
>   your love to me was wonderful,
>   passing the love of women.
>
> (2 Sam 1:26)

Some exegetes have rightly suggested that the translation of the verse "your love to me was wonderful" should be "your love to me was miraculous," since the category of "wonder" had, at that time, a marked religious significance. It designated the prodigious activity of God in history. Friendship can be, and often is, a perfect miracle.

There is one further detail to be emphasized in the history of this friendship, namely David's question: "Is there still anyone left of the house of Saul to whom I may show kindness for Jonathan's sake?" (2 Sam 9:1). David became a protector of the descendants of Jonathan. His son and his grandson used to eat at David's table, like any one of the king's sons (2 Sam 9:11).

DAVID AND BARZILLAI

When Absalom rebelled against David, his father, and David had to flee, we are told about his friendship with the octogenarian Barzillai, a man from the region of Gilead. The most difficult moments in life are often the most fruitful in signs of hope that happen by pure grace. The pact of friendship comes about, to begin with, in the form of compassion and hospitality. "The troops are hungry and weary and thirsty in the wilderness" (2 Sam 17:29), said Barzillai as he set about helping David and his companions. However, the initial step of offering material aid turned into a deeper friendship, the essence of which consisted in the pleasure of each other's company. A compassionate gesture is not always capable of generating a friendship, but it is lovely when it does do so. David suggested to Barzillai: "Come over with me, and I will provide for you in Jerusalem" (19:33). But Barzillai preferred to spend his remaining days in his own land, and asked David to accept instead the company of one of his sons. "The king kissed Barzillai and blessed him, and [Barzillai] returned to his own home" (19:39). The patrimony of friendship is full of these endings.

ELISHA AND THE SHUNAMITE WOMAN

This friendship began with an invitation to share a meal. "One day Elisha was passing through Shunem, where a wealthy woman lived, who urged him to have a meal. So whenever he passed that way, he would stop there for a meal" (2 Kgs 4:8). Sharing at table led to greater knowledge of and greater concern for each other. The family who had befriended the prophet decided to build a small roof chamber for him, and it is moving to read the detailed description with "a bed, a table, a chair, and a lamp, so that he can stay there whenever he comes to us (4:10). In order to reward the Shunamite woman and her husband, Elisha promised her that she would bear a child: "At this season, in due time, you shall embrace a son" (4:16). In addition to the miracle, which is typical of the activity of the prophet, we see here the daily and equally transforming miracle that is brought about by friendship. But here too it is important for us to reflect on the very human way in which the story is told. When a servant of the prophet wants to drive the woman away when she is in tears, Elisha reprimands him: "Let her alone, for she is in bitter distress" (4:27). Friends do not protect only our laughter. They also give us the time to weep when we need to do so.

JOB'S FRIENDS

The story of Job is so well known that it has become an icon of human suffering. Job sought to live an upright life before God and men, and he was harshly tormented by the experience of evil, an unmitigated evil that descended upon him like an absurd obscenity that can in no way be accounted for. Job's complaint is a protest, the opposite of a prayer, a refusal to submit that collides with all attempts at explanation. Then Job attacks God's silence in order to say to him, "Let me know why you contend against me" (Job 10:2). There are also three friends who come to discuss things with him. Anyone who has been tried by suffering, or has suffered together with someone, well knows how at such times, wordy explanations are felt to be both useless and almost as scandalous as an insult. It may well be that in no other situation than that of suffering are we aware of the rhetoric of consolation that is repeated mechanically and, in the last analysis, insincere. But Eliphaz, Bildad, and Zophar speak at length. Gianfranco Ravasi has written:

> The three friends are also three representatives of theological and ideological reality. They embody three fundamental answers: that of wisdom, of prophecy and of law. They are the theologians, the philosophers. They are all those who throughout the history of humanity try to find an answer to the questions that are asked: Why is there evil? Does it make sense to believe in the absurdity of suffering? And they produce their carefully concocted ideological recipes. The book of Job then becomes a fierce polemic against facile ideologies unconnected with reality, concocted in some laboratory or other to such an extent that they seem to come from a marble tower, with no means of contact with the real world.

For this reason, Job's reply to what his friends have to say is "What you know, I also know; I am not inferior to you. But I would speak to the Almighty, and I desire to argue my case with God" (13:2–3). And this is what happens. Among other things, Job's theology of protest teaches us that friendship can never falsify the search for meaning, even the most demanding and solitary.

"MY FRIEND HAD A VINEYARD"

One of the loveliest biblical reflections on friendship is the "Song of the Friend" that we find in the Book of Isaiah (5:1–7): "Let me sing for my beloved my love-song concerning his vineyard." The vineyard is clearly allegorical, as the text itself shows: "For the vineyard of the LORD of hosts is the house of Israel, and the people of Judah are his pleasant planting." However, the friends are real people: the Prophet and God.

The most striking thing about this astonishing poem is that the Prophet places himself by God's side as a friend, comforting him at a time of trial, entering into a pact with him at a time of crisis ("What more was there to do for my vineyard that I have not done in it?" [5:4]). It is true that it is God who decides the fate of a vineyard of which every care had been taken, but which produces only wild grapes. But God seeks our help in reaching his decision ("Judge between me and my vineyard" [5:3]). In the mystery that is friendship, we already see in Isaiah what, for example, one of our contemporaries, Etty Hillesum, was to say explicitly: "It is we who must help you [O God] and in helping you help ourselves. And that is all we can manage these days and also all that really matters."

JESUS AND LAZARUS

Friendship plays a considerable and fundamental part in the picture that the New Testament presents to us of Jesus. His relationship with the disciples was clearly one of friendship: "I do not call you servants, for the servant does not know what his master is doing; but I have called you friends" (John 15:15, alt. translation). If we are to go by the accusation that was made against him, "friend of tax collectors and sinners" (Luke 7:34), his relationship with sinners needs to be seen in the same light. But the only person in the whole of the New Testament who is specifically described as a friend of Jesus is

Lazarus of Bethany, the brother of Mary and Martha. These three together can all be described as "friends," and I shall have more to say about Martha and Mary later on. For now, what interests us is the question: In what way does the story of the friendship between Jesus and Lazarus as it is portrayed in the Gospel cast light on the mystery that is an integral part of all friendship?

It seems to me that four aspects stand out clearly:

1. *To rely on one's friend.* Mary and Martha warn Jesus that Lazarus is sick: "Lord, he whom you love is ill" (John 11:3), and they are sure that he will come, even at great inconvenience. The worried disciples said to him, "The Jews were just now trying to stone you, and are you going there again?" (John 11:8). But the truth is that Jesus is on his way to Bethany like anyone who cannot not be with his friend at a time of illness or grief.

2. *To weep for one's friend.* To rejoice with the joys of another as if they were one's own; and, in the same way, to sympathize with him or her at a time of pain or sorrow. Jesus is deeply moved (as the Gospel text itself tells us twice: John 11:33, 38) and weeps (John 11:35). This image of Jesus weeping at the death of his friend tells us things that words themselves cannot express.

3. *To accompany one's friend to the end (and beyond).* The death of Lazarus opens the way for the divine revelation of Jesus: "I believe that you are the Messiah, the Son of God, the one coming into the world" (John 11:27), declares Martha. But every friend is charged with the mission of repeating Jesus' words, bearing witness to them: "Your brother will rise again" (John 11:23). How can one do this: keeping the memory, keeping alive communion with the spiritual patrimony

represented by the life of one's friend and believing in the triumph of life over death prefigured by Jesus himself?

4. *To go back to one's friend.* Friendship, in fact, is fed by a multiplicity of meetings and returns. After the ultimate experience suffered by Lazarus, Jesus visits him again, in order to savor the sweetness of friendship and its fragrance. "Jesus came to Bethany, the home of Lazarus, whom he had raised from the dead. There they gave a dinner for him. Martha served, and Lazarus was one of those at the table with him. Mary took a pound of costly perfume made of pure nard, anointed Jesus' feet, and wiped them with her hair. The house was filled with the fragrance of the perfume" (John 12:1–3).

PAUL AND THE MARRIED COUPLE: PRISCILLA AND AQUILA

Nowadays, Pauline studies rightly emphasize the contribution made by a wide range of fellow workers, thereby overcoming the idea of the apostle as a solitary hero. In fact, throughout Paul's extensive missionary activity, a crucial role was played by the network, the teamwork, the complementarity (including that of temperaments!), the delegations, and, of course, the friendship. St. Paul lived many stories of friendship. Here we will reflect on just one, the friendship between Paul and the married couple Priscilla and Aquila. References to this friendship occur in a number of New Testament texts: in the Letter to the Romans, to the Corinthians, the second Letter to Timothy, and in the Acts of the Apostles. Aquila was a Hebrew and a native of Pontus (in present-day Turkey), although he had a Latin name. The first information we are given is that he was living in Rome, where he had presumably met his wife Priscilla, also referred to by the diminutive Prisca. When the emperor Claudius promulgated an edict expelling all Jews living in Rome, the two, though they were already Christians, had taken refuge in the Greek city of Corinth, which is where they first met Paul. As both they and Paul practiced the same trade, that of tent-making, "[Paul] stayed with them, and they worked together" (Acts 18:3). Thus his friendship is wide-ranging and based on hospitality. From Corinth they travelled together to Ephesus, the other strategic center for evangelization on Paul's preaching circuit. In fact, we see Priscilla and Aquila in Ephesus dedicated to the formation of a new convert named Apollos (Acts 18:26). In both Corinth and Ephesus, these two friends constituted an affective background of solicitude and collaboration for the Apostle. When Paul wrote to the Corinthians from Ephesus, we know that Pricilla and Aquila were with him, for they are mentioned among the list of greetings at the end of the letter: "Aquila and Prisca, together with the church in their house, greet you warmly in the Lord" (1 Cor 16:19). It is interesting that their house is referred to as a "house-church" where the community was accustomed to meet for the Word and the Breaking of Bread.

When Claudius's edit was withdrawn, the couple returned to Rome, but distance did not affect either the friendship or the sense of gratitude. In the letter he wrote to the Christians in Rome, Paul speaks highly of them: "Greet Prisca and Aquila, who work with me in Christ Jesus, and who risked their necks for my life, to whom not only I give thanks, but also all the churches of the Gentiles" (Rom 16:3–4). The greeting sent to them by Paul in 2 Timothy 4:19, "greet Prisca and Aquila," is a further sign that true friends never forget one another.

3

THINKING ABOUT FRIENDSHIP

A multiplicity of terms has been used in both Latin and Greek to describe the experience of love; whereas, in both cases, friendship is presented predominantly by means of two terms: *philia* in Greek and *amicitia* in Latin. To begin with, however, the meaning of both these terms was very much part of the field of love. Only gradually was friendship perceived as a reality that needed to be defined autonomously. Originally, the word *philos* meant "dear, beloved" in a sense that was very close to that of the possessive "my." In Homer, what characterizes friendship is this belonging to and nearness as immediate forms of possession. It was only at the end of a semantic evolution that the idea of possession was diluted into a notion of affection that overcomes all bonds. The same is true of the Latin word for friendship. The terms *amor* and *amicitia* are both derived from the root *am*, which in Vulgar Latin denotes "mother (*amma*)" and "nurse (*mama*)." Thus, in friendship, there would be the idea of a mother's love or, in other words, love as an essential structure of existence.

What is certain is that, from very ancient times up to the present, friendship has constituted a permanent challenge for thought. Giorgio Agamben, for example, reminds us that the close relationship between friendship and philosophy is so deep that philosophy includes the notion of *philos* or "friend" in its very name. Philosophy is not only the cultivation of wisdom. It is also a question to be debated between friends and it is thus a concrete exercise in friendship. It is important for us to recover something of the history of thought about friendship in order to perceive that many questions that we live at our own personal level in fact constitute part of universal problems. What can be said about friendship? What is its language? How is it constructed and deconstructed? Is it an autonomous human expression or can it only be used when linked to other landscapes? Is friendship always a good thing? Let us make our way through the questions that friendship provokes. We may well be able to live friendship better if we accept the invitation to make contact with the thinking that it has evoked over the centuries.

MOVING FROM THE SENSITIVE TO THE INTELLIGIBLE

Let us begin with the Greeks. One of Plato's works, *The Symposium* (*The Banquet*), may help us to understand what distinguishes the concept of love from that of friendship in the Greco-Latin culture to which we still belong. The work has a theatrical setting that gives it great vivacity: Apollodorus is urged by a friend to describe a banquet that had been held in the house of Agathon and at which Pausanias, Eryximachos, Aristophanes, and Socrates, among others, had been present. The thinking proceeds in the form of a dialogue in which each of those present will be given a chance to state his ideas about love. What emerges from the conversation is the drawing of a kind of map very much centered on sensitive and passionate love. The desire for love, it is stated at one point, is also mixed up with a longing to recover a unity that has been lost. In the beginning, we were cut in two and instead of one whole, there are now two halves. Thus, through love, each half seeks what corresponds to it. But for Plato, love is also a movement from the sensitive to the intelligible, from the beauty of bodies to the beauty of ideas, from eros to friendship. This idea is explained to us in the words of Diotima, who declared: "There is indeed a theory that lovers are people who are in search of the other half of themselves….But according to my view of the matter, love is not desire either of the half or of the whole….Love is the desire for the perpetual possession of the good" (205e/206a). How does this come about? By a process that moves from the particular to the universal, from the physical to the spiritual, from the beautiful to the good. It is a way of intellective ascesis that causes us to pass from the beauty of a particular body to the beauty of all bodies, from beautiful bodies to the beauty of customs and knowledge until, by means of these, one perceives that the truth of the beautiful, taken to its ultimate limits, opens us to the beauty of wisdom.

THE DISINTERESTED SEARCH FOR THE GOOD

Aristotle, for his part, pays great attention to friendship in his *Nicomachean Ethics*, and he speaks of it not as a move toward the intelligible, but as a very concrete civic virtue. "Friendship seems to hold states together," he comments (bk. 8, chap. 1, 22–23). With this concept, the philosopher identifies and establishes a hierarchy of various forms of friendship: (1) Love for the sake of utility, which is based on the advantage each one may derive from a relationship where there is mutual sharing; (2) love for the sake of pleasure, based principally on the pleasure one may derive from the company of the other; (3) virtuous friendship, which seeks above all the good of the other. Only this last, in fact, can be regarded as a virtue that, when it exists, reveals the excellence of those who practice it. "Now these are most truly friends, for they seek for their friends the good that they seek for themselves. And this is so because they appreciate their friends for what they are in themselves and not for incidental reasons. Their friendship lasts as long as they are good, and goodness is an enduring thing. Each one is a good without qualification for his friend" (bk. 8, chap. 3, 10–14).

According to Aristotle, the disinterested search for the good of the other, an equivalence between the love we bestow on others and the love we have for ourselves, sincere concern, the lack of any heartthrob-like or passionate attraction are all indications of an authentic friendship. Complete equality, reciprocity, and nondependence also form part of the grammar of love. Only in the recognition of equality, only when the reciprocity is free, can the friendship ultimately be firmly established. And it demands that each of the two is completely autonomous.

SEEK NOTHING SHAMEFUL, GRANT NOTHING SHAMEFUL

Cicero composed his treatise *De Amicitia* in a particularly crucial period, namely that of the meteoric rise of Caesar and his assassination at the hands of his protégé and friend, Marcus Brutus, in March of the year 44 BC. Thus Cicero's text, in a sense, foreshadows the historical situation at that time. The literary model of his treatise is that of Plato's *Dialogues*, and the point of departure is the posthumous evocation of the qualities of a friend. The memory of this friendship constitutes the substance of the text. For Cicero, apart from wisdom, there is nothing better than friendship, defined as perfect agreement in all things human and divine, accompanied by goodwill and affection. "What is sweeter than to have someone with whom you may dare discuss anything as if you were communing with yourself?" Friendship, however, is born of virtue and not of necessity. Its rule is this: "Neither ask dishonorable things, nor do them, if asked." The benefits derived from it are not to be looked upon as the principal motive for its existence. Since the choice of friends is not a simple matter, it must be done with care. Cicero recommends that one should choose those that are firm and constant, but he really only believes in a friendship that proves itself such over time.

ONLY A WISE PERSON KNOWS HOW TO LOVE

Seneca did not leave us his conception of friendship in a treatise but in a series of letters written to an addressee who was, at the same time, a friend called Lucilius. This is in line with his basic premise. Rather than define a friend, his aim was to understand the life and duties of friendship. To live as a friend is more important than to describe what a friend is. Like Aristotle and Cicero, Seneca too begins by classifying friendship as a virtue, but the power of his stoic ideals takes him further, and he ends by identifying friendship with wisdom. "Only the wise person knows how to love, only the wise person is a friend" [*Solus sapiens scit amare, solus sapiens amicus est*]. Seneca protests against the organizing of friends into classes. A man who is good should choose wise people as his friends, and place little trust in social power and prestige. Hence, he urges Lucilius not to seek his friends either in the senate or the market place, when he can find better people at home or among his slaves.

BECAUSE HE WAS HE. BECAUSE I WAS ME.

Montaigne's definition of his friendship with Étienne de la Boétie is well known: "In the friendship of which I speak, souls mingle and blend with each other so completely that they efface the seam that joined them to such an extent that they cannot find it again. If you want me to say why I loved him, I can only reply by saying: 'Because he was he. Because I was me.' [*Parce que c'était lui, parce que c'était moi*]." Montaigne does not seek to know or to say why La Boétie was his friend. The absence of explanations expresses the nature of friendship as a kind of matrix. It does not have any particular aim. Friendship can have no other purpose than itself. One must not confuse friendship with the respect that is typical of parental relationships and, in the same way, it is not legitimate to compare it with erotic love. For Montaigne, love is a communion of spirit, a kind of union of souls. It is an inexpressible, intransitive, absolute relationship that does not seek to modify the other or to be modified by him or her. It is not a question of the meeting of two desires, but of two fullnesses. It is in this sense that we are to understand the dictum: "Because he was he. Because I was me."

George Steiner has recently revisited Montaigne's text and pointed out that, in fact, external circumstances or existential attributes are quite irrelevant, and they are nonnegotiable whether it is a question of physical charm, social compatibility, or pragmatic alliances, still less of those stories of love or of hatred that at times are handed down in families. Incongruence does not count when it is a question of friendship. What we know is that, without friendship, a woman or a man would be living as if they were exiled. Friendship authorizes us to say, "I am because you are."

MY FRIEND IS NOTHING OTHER THAN ONE HALF OF MYSELF

A treatise on friendship nearly always conceals the story of a friendship. One of the most extraordinary is the friendship that united the Jesuit missionary Matteo Ricci and the Chinese prince Qian Zhai. They first met in 1595. This is how Matteo Ricci expresses his memory of this meeting:

I, Matteo, having come by sea from the great West entered China admiring the noble virtues of the Son of Heaven of the great Mings and the teachings handed down by the ancient kings....In the spring of this year, by crossing the mountain and navigating the rivers, I reached Jinling where, to my great joy, I was able to admire the light of the great kingdom....Even before I completed my journey, I went to Nanchang....For this reason I went to see the prince of Jian'an, who did not ignore me but allowed me to make a profound inclination, made me sit in the seat reserved for guests, offered me sweet wine and prepared a great feast for me.

[When the feasting was over], the prince rose from his place, came over to me and taking me by the hands, said: "When noble men of great virtue condescend to visit my land, I never fail to invite them to dine, and treat them as friends and pay them honor. The great West is the country of morality and justice: I would like to hear what is said there about friendship."

This gave rise to the book *On Friendship: One Hundred Maxims for a Chinese Prince*, which met with enormous success in the China of that time and is a genuine classic on the theme, in addition to the delightful detail that it was the first work written in Chinese by someone from the West. The treatise presents one hundred quotations taken from the whole of European thought, Greco-Latin and Christian. Two things were clear to Ricci: (1) The dialogue between the West and the East needed to rest on a basis of mutual knowledge and friendship. (2) Only by means of friendship would it be possible to hand on the gospel in the very different context and human outlook represented by the "Middle Empire." The way in which Matteo Ricci's precious little book begins is quite unforgettable: "My friend is nothing other than one half of myself; or rather, he is another me. For this reason, I must look upon my friend as being myself."

WHERE THERE ARE NO PROPERTY RIGHTS

In his *The Gay Science*, Nietzsche denounces the love that is thought of as a desire to take possession of the other and a strategy of domination. For him, the territory of such a love is "possession." "It is the love of sex for sex that can be seen most clearly as a desire for possession: the one who loves wants to be sole possessor of the object of his or her desire, wants to exercise an absolute power over both the soul and the body of the other, wants to be the only one loved, establish him-/herself to reign in the other's soul as the highest and the most desirable." But there are other kinds of love that do not give in to this urge to possess, respecting the distance between the I and the Thou. Nietzsche wrote: "There does in fact exist, here and there on earth, a kind of prolongation of love in which the desire that the two people concerned feel for each other gives rise to a new desire, a new longing, a new superior mutual thirst, an ideal that is above and beyond both. But who is there who knows this love? Who has actually lived it? Its true name is *friendship*" (n. 14). In friendship, we are one with the other and we are also one for the other, while maintaining a certain distance. Friends do not diminish one another, they do not juxtapose themselves one against the other, nor do they substitute themselves one for the other. Friendship is a way of exposing oneself to the other, but it is an exposure that does not impinge on the other's reserve, does not invade the other's privacy. Friendship not only remains silent; it is protected by silence.

PARALLEL LINES THAT MEET IN INFINITY

According to Simone Weil, the love that Christ urges us to practice with his "love one another" is a love that is absolutely anonymous and universal, that is, charity. Friendship is an exception in that it represents a preference for one particular human being. But it does not cease to be a miraculous expression of the supernatural in us. It would be impossible for us to live friendship purely if God did not allow us to combine that which, naturally, emerges as separate and contrary: on the one hand, our need for others and, on the other, the absolute necessity of respect both for the other's autonomy and for our own. There is no friendship except one in which a certain distance is maintained. Weil explains this as follows:

> Friendship is a miracle by which a person consents to view from a certain distance, and without coming any nearer, the very being who is necessary to him or her as food. It requires the strength of soul that Eve did not have; and yet she had no need of the fruit. If she had been hungry at the moment when she looked at the fruit, and if in spite of that she had remained looking at it indefinitely without taking one step toward it, she would have performed a miracle analogous to that of perfect friendship. (from "Essay on Friendship," in *Waiting for God*)

Pure friendship is an image of the perfect love of the Trinity. It is impossible for two human beings to be one and in spite of this to respect scrupulously the distance that separates them unless God is present in each of them. For this reason, friends are parallel lines that only meet in infinity.

WHAT SEPARATES BECOMES RELATIONSHIP

Maurice Blanchot defines friendship as one of the most fruitful situations in the human condition. I hope for nothing from a friend, or rather, I hope for everything insofar as, by its radical difference, his/her existence enables me to exist. Friendship is the acceptance of a pure interval that, from me to this other who is my friend, measures everything there is between us. The sweetness of friendship, however, is equivalent to its most unyielding rigor: my friend is this neighbor who does not cease to be furthest away from me. According to Blanchot:

> Friendship, this relationship without dependence, without episode, yet which contains all the simplicity of life, passes by way of the recognition of the common strangeness that does not allow us to speak of our friends but only to speak to them, not to make of them a topic of conversations (or of essays), but the movement of understanding in which, speaking to us, they reserve, even on the most familiar terms, an infinite distance, the fundamental separation on the basis of which what separates becomes relation. (From *Amitié* by Maurice Blanchot. English translation by Elizabeth Rottenberg)

FRIENDS, THERE ARE NO FRIENDS

"My friends, there are no friends" is an enigmatic maxim that tradition attributes to Aristotle, and which, while seeming to invoke friendship ("friends"), at the same time seems also to deny it ("there are no friends"). It appears in a developed form in the work of both Montaigne and Nietzsche, who perhaps took it from a chapter on the biography of Aristotle attributed to Diogenes Laertius. And this maxim was used by Jacques Derrida to write his *Politics of Friendship*.

There is a curious story that is told by a philosopher friend of Derrida's, the Italian Giorgio Agamben. He relates how, when Derrida was still in the process of organizing the academic seminar that was to give rise to the book, they discussed at length a philological problem connected with the phrase. After investigating various versions, Agamben managed to reconstruct the history of the phrase and perceived that the enigmatic maxim had in fact been created by a copyist's error. Instead of "My friends, there are no friends," the original was probably "anybody who has (many) friends, has no real friend." Agamben immediately told Jacques Derrida what he had discovered and was amazed when, on reading *The Politics of Friendship*, he could find no reference to their conversation. It was not due to forgetfulness that Derrida continued to use the "My friends, there are no friends" version. For the strategy of his reflection, it was essential for friendship to be simultaneously both recommended and questioned. This is the really useful contribution: questioning the centrality that the paradigm of fraternity occupies in the great debates concerning friendship.

In fact, when one conceives of friendship as a process of the equivalence of subjectivities—in which friendship is reduced to a machine producing identical subjects—one has also to be aware of the risk of excluding the other and the different that slyly manages to dominate. The concept of friendship as a symbiotic relationship, or a "fusion of souls" along Montaigne's lines, is denounced as a danger that, in the course of history, has so often resulted in the logic of intolerance, doing away with singularity and reducing the other to oneself. Instead, Derrida proposes a rupture, suggesting that we should think of friendship without the prerogative of closeness or intimacy. In this way there would come about a friendship turned toward dissymmetry, the irreducible precedence of the other (in his or her otherness) in a democracy still to come.

4

LIVING IN FRIENDSHIP
WITH GOD

There is a passage in the Gospel of St. John (3:8), that is normally translated as follows: "The wind blows where it wills, and you hear the sound of it, but you do not know whence it comes or whither it goes; so it is with every one who is born of the Spirit" (RSV). The Greek term for Spirit is *pneuma*, but *pneuma* also means "wind." This presents the translator with the problem of opting for either one term or the other. Having decided to translate *pneuma* as "wind," what are we saying? That the trajectory of the one who is born of the Spirit, that is, the trajectory of the believer, the history of believing, is open to the unforeseen. It is like the wind, we hear the sound of it, but we do not know where it comes from nor where it is going. The emphasis is thus on the believer. It is he or she who has a life that is in the open and in the unforeseeable.

But if, as the Vulgate does, we opt for "the Spirit blows where it wills," the element that is unforeseen ceases to be the trajectory of the believer and moves over to the side of God. It is the Spirit that is unforeseeable; it is the voice of the Spirit of God that I hear, but I do not know where it comes from nor whither it goes. The Spirit is thus to be found in the open, in the unsaid, the unpronounceable, the uncatalogued, the untrodden. It is the Divine Spirit that becomes the ongoing manifestation of the unedited.

ACCEPTING THE ENIGMA

We are unforeseeable. At times we look at ourselves in the mirror and, even without actually saying it, we repeat that line of Rimbaud's, "I am another." Who is this who is looking at me in the mirror? We look at ourselves and there is this strangeness of being that is always there: But am I really like that? What road is this? What are these times that are within me? We are also a secret for ourselves and we have to accept ourselves like this. We are an enigma, a question, and we have to accept this. Otherwise, there will be no peace for us. We will always be living in a state of division and conflict. Hence, there is a moment at which we need to say: "Very well then, that's how things are. I do not explain, I do not conceive, I do not plan, but that's how things are, and I will do something with this."

But where God is concerned, it is much more difficult to conceive of him as being unforeseeable. For we are greatly consoled by the thought that God is here. That we encounter him here, that by following this path, we will undoubtedly reach him. There are times when we like to think that God is among the things we are tidying up, part of our interior dispositions, in the thoughts in our heads. We like to know that he is and is in a particular way. We run the risk of living our relationship with God not as a friendship but as a habit.

RECOGNIZE THAT GOD LIVES IN ME. BUT HOW?

There are two images in the New Testament that evoke far distant echoes from the history of Israel at the time of the prophets, and that are used to describe the relationship of friendship with the Spirit. Possibly the best known of these, which may well have been with us since we were children and forms our own way of conceiving of God, is the image of outpouring. We have this in chapter 2 of the Acts of the Apostles: the Apostles were together and the Spirit descended upon them. Hence, when we think of the Holy Spirit of God, we think of something that comes down upon us and is combined with that which we are. It is in us. In other words, it is in me and in what I am. This outpouring or effusion, as the word *effusion* indicates, is a kind of fusion. And I feel that God in me makes me to be, gives me courage for the battle, wisdom for the word, joy for the dance.

Both the Gospels and the letters of St. Paul are full of expressions that point in this direction, bearing witness to the fact that the experience of friendship with God, in the Person of his Holy Spirit, is a fusional experience. For example, in the work of Luke (his Gospel and the Acts of the Apostles), the Angel says to Mary, "The Holy Spirit will come upon you" (Luke 1:35); Elizabeth, on welcoming Mary "was filled with the Holy Spirit" (Luke 1:41); after the Lord's Resurrection, Peter spoke to the authorities and to the people "filled with the Holy Spirit" (Acts 7:55); in the house of Cornelius "the Holy Spirit fell upon all who heard the word" (Acts 10:44), and more. This "being filled with the Holy Spirit" is an ongoing experience in the construction of the Christian way.

In this image of fusion, the contours of singularity are, as it were, exceeded, thereby establishing a coincidence between the believing subject and what that subject believes. I believe, and the One in whom I believe makes me be. There is no distance between what the subject believes and what the subject is; there is an indivisible communion. It is in this sense that the entire liturgy of baptism speaks of baptism in the Spirit. The believers are wrapped, clothed, as if the Spirit were now their skin.

It is on the basis of this image, for example, that we are called upon to understand the discourses of Jesus on the Spirit in the fourth Gospel. Jesus makes use of all-embracing language when he says the Spirit will teach you all things (see John 14:26). It is not a question of teaching something, some particular aspect that is missing. No, the Spirit will teach everything. He will teach completely.

And how is the Spirit described? He is described as fire,

as a mighty wind, a light, a soul, a courage to speak out, a breath that we need in order to be. This image, which is also an experience of the Spirit that I think all of us have—for at a certain moment we feel that the friendship with God penetrates us completely—certainly leads us to the truth of God, but describing it as an experience of fullness.

FRIENDSHIP AS AN EXPERIENCE OF COINCIDENCE

These moments of fullness find a basis in the Old Testament tradition concerning the status of the people of God. What is it that turns Israel into a people of the covenant? Is it to have a law, a constitution with ten commandments, a covenant, a promise? It is all this, undoubtedly, but rounded off by an outpouring of the Spirit, by an experience of God himself. "I will pour out my spirit on all flesh; your sons and your daughters shall prophesy, your old men shall dream dreams, and your young men shall see visions. Even on the male and female slaves, in those days, I will pour out my spirit" (Joel 2:28–29). There is this experience as a condition for becoming a people of God.

Normally, when the Spirit of God appears in the Old Testament, it manifests itself in a spectacular way: there is an upheaval in nature, there are earthquakes, volcanoes, fierce winds. We might say the manifestation of God provokes a kind of alteration in the cosmic order, introducing a new experience, a new cycle, a new time. In the New Testament, everything is purified. The experience of contact with God continues to be an experience of fusion, but expressed in a more intimate and naked way. When the disciples receive the Holy Spirit, they are in a house, in an unknown street in the city (Acts 2:1), not in front of a fiery mountain (see Exod 19:16, 18). The Holy Spirit descends on them without any untoward natural phenomenon. The Spirit is now given in the course of the day, in our humanity; it is given in a delicate, interior, and hidden way. The mighty wind that filled the house where they were sitting can in no way be compared to the atmospheric upheaval described in the Book of Exodus. Let us have a look at this text in Acts 2:1–4: "When the day of Pentecost had come, they were all together in one place. And suddenly from heaven there came a sound like the rush of a violent wind, and it filled the entire house where they were sitting. Divided tongues, as of fire, appeared among them, and a tongue rested on each of them. All of them were filled with the Holy Spirit and began to speak in other languages, as the Spirit gave them ability." "To be filled" is an experience of fusion, of being carried away, of being filled with the Spirit. In the Gospel of St. John (14:16–17), Jesus says: "I will ask the Father, and he will give you another Advocate, to be with you for ever. This is the Spirit of truth, whom the world cannot receive, because it neither sees him nor knows him. You know him, because he abides with you, and he will be in you." Notice that the Spirit of God is not merely close to us, the Spirit is "in us." Here we have, once again, the fusional experience to describe this friendship. And the same applies to the spiritual testament of the Apostle St. Paul that we find in the Letter to the Romans (8:26): "Likewise the Spirit helps us in our weakness; for we do not know how to pray as we ought, but that very Spirit intercedes with sighs too deep for words." This is an experience of friendship in God that bursts forth as spiritual intimacy: we feel that the Spirit is filling us, the Spirit makes us be.

FRIENDSHIP AS AN EXPERIENCE OF DIFFERENCE

But if the Spirit of God is in us in a fusional form, how are we to understand those moments when it seems that the Spirit is not there? How to understand the desert, the times of weakness and scarcity, the times of lack of inspiration, the dark nights, the asking of questions, the times of doubt and discouragement, the sharp thorn of our lack of enthusiasm? If the Spirit is always with us, if there really is this almost maternal fusion, as if we were still in our mother's womb, how are we to understand and accept these states that we experience? The translation that tells us that "the Spirit blows where it wills and you hear its voice, but you do not know where it comes from nor where it is going," is also, in fact, a necessary translation.

Friendship with the Spirit of God happens in two ways in our lives: either by means of this experience of fusion, or by means of its opposite, that of differentiation. Either God's friendship fills us, or we seem to be empty of it, because God is always other. I do not control the Spirit of God; I am not its master or lord. It is God who, at all times, is absolutely other. As the theologian Joseph Moingt says: "The fact that the Spirit is here, is in each one of us, does not mean that he cannot also be somewhere else, since he is present both in closeness and in distance. Often, the Spirit is in what is familiar and, equally often, the Spirit is in what is strange or different. He is always over and above and he does not allow himself to be possessed or closed in, neither does he remain in a place except to go further without ever withdrawing from where he has come from."

The Spirit of God does not abandon us, but neither does he settle down in us. The request that Peter made to Jesus at the time of the Transfiguration, "Lord, let us make here three tents," is a request that Jesus does not wish to hear, as he immediately tells them to go back down the mountain. God is a pilgrim; he moves; he is always different. And we, how do we receive the friendship of God? We receive it both in our fidelity to it, to its repetition, to the prolongation of the gesture and of the place, to the memory, as well as in the differentiation, the risk, the unexpected, the original, the extraordinary, the new.

THE SPIRIT IS THE THIRD

The Holy Spirit is the third in the order of the Trinity. God is Trinity. If we reflect on our human experience, the third is the one who upsets the projection of equivalence. Two are a symbol of reciprocity and of fusion: in the two I have one project. I am one plus one. There is an element of diversity. A community comprising two persons is very different from one comprising three. This is because the third brings with himself or herself the truth of a relationship that cannot be the project of an I and a You. The third forces us into an open relationship, one that is not focused. The Spirit is this third Person. The mystery of God is threefold.

We very often pray as follows: "Come Lord and give me, help me, strengthen me, comfort me." Obviously, the Lord comes. But I must not forget that God is the One who is different, his Spirit points out for me the way forward that I have not yet embarked on, the one I am about to embark on, the one that lies in wait for me, the one I do not know. This differentiation of the Spirit—making us perceive that God is unforeseeable—purifies our friendship with God. We need to be purified of the fixations that so often tone down our spirituality. There is, in fact, a sense in which we tame or tone down the image of God. We already know so much, we are always expecting a friendship lived as closeness. And yet God is also in the uncomfortableness of the search, in the demands and the delay of the journey, in the anguish of doubt. He is in the certainty that he is the Other, irreducibly Other. That he is not in me, that he does not abide in me, that I am not God. This makes us responsible and adult in the construction of the friendship that is the faith. And it makes it not into a foreseeable search for consolation but an open-ended search for a friend, God.

OUR FRIEND IS A STRANGER

The greatest mistake in the spiritual life is to live on the things of God and not on God himself; to live exclusively on those things that bring us consolation. There is a striking passage in the Book of Exodus (4:24–26). It is a story that may strike us as terrible, but it is there and we have to find a meaning for it. Moses had reached a stopping place on his journey, and during the night the Lord came and fought with him and tried to kill him. We read this story and we say to ourselves: "I'm sorry, but this is nonsense." This God who speaks to Moses as a man speaks to his friend, this God who reveals his beauty to Moses, suddenly turns on him and does battle with him? What can that possibly mean? Whatever it means it does, in fact, remain mysterious. But in all its mystery it tells us that God is God and at times we forget this. We forget that God is Other, God is transcendent and I have to remain in my place. There are in fact times when we take the closeness for granted. We get God mixed up in all the trappings of our lives. No, we must not take God for granted. God is a question. God is a wonder. God is a stranger, the One who, as John the Baptist said about Jesus: "Among you stands one whom you do not know" (John 1:26). Our friend is always a stranger.

THE VISIBLE IS ONLY
THE HIDDEN EDGE

The Brazilian theologian and psychoanalyst Ruben Alves has written something that I find very interesting. In describing his own consulting room, he says:

> In my consulting room there are two pictures, two paintings, one of which portrays a luminous landscape with very sharp colors, where the flowers are

clearly visible against a green background with mountains whose tops reach up to the blue of the sky. When they see it for the first time, the people who come into the room exclaim: "How lovely!" But they say no more because the transcendence says all there is to be said and so the conversation comes to an end. The other picture portrays a wood, thick and impenetrable with shadowy figures, the trees indistinguishable and a solitary pathway that disappears in a widespread and mysterious mist....When they look at it, people halt in their tracks, they do not know what to think but, after a silence, there comes the beginning of a long conversation: "I wonder," they say to me, "what there is behind the mist, behind the trees, hidden in the darkness?" Really, here the visible is only the ragged edge which suggests the invisible, the unsayable, the unknown.

Very often, the way we speak about God uses him up completely. This is so when our friendship with God is not deep enough. But at other times, our prayer, our search, our knowledge of, and our savoring of God is no more than the hidden edge that suggests the unknown. Without this, faith becomes an ideology, it ceases to be a meeting and the meeting of friends; it ceases to be a search, and quickly turns into a list of rules and rites. It ceases to be that place of discovery and rediscovery that we are. Our belief in a very stable knowledge plunges us into a kind of idolatry. We have to keep on asking: What is it that brings me closest to God? Knowing or not knowing? The search for a sense of security at all costs or the hopeful search for a friendship that is growing to maturity?

5

I HAVE CALLED YOU FRIENDS

Jesus had friends, and friendship was a marked feature in the construction of his way. He associated friends with his mission, making of friendship a place for the recognition of himself and of friendship with God. If we accept Timothy Radcliffe's definition of friendship, which he describes as "the immense risk of letting ourselves be seen by others in all our vulnerability, handing ourselves over to them," Jesus, more than any other person, is entitled to be known as "the friend."

The atmosphere of the Gospels leaves no room for doubt. Jesus developed his mission outside the traditional sacred space: he trod a path well away from the temple, choosing religiously neutral places such as houses, the shore of the lake, the roadway, places principally associated with the activity of human beings. But it was not only a question of new places that were closer to people's daily lives; it was also a question of new gestures and new words. The indignation of those who accused Jesus of being the friend of publicans and sinners because he sat at table and shared meals with them (see Luke 7:34), is in fact an indication of Jesus' unusual way of doing things. The culture of his day recommended "separation," whereas Jesus stood out as a prophet of relationship and friendship.

Jesus also gave a new meaning to some old words. The vocabulary of love and friendship is not the same after Jesus as before. Let us look at this typical term for friendship, the Greek word *philia*, and its semantics. In John's Gospel, the term occurs six times in applications that are decisive for the development of friendship. The love of agape is the love of charity, a divinised love; in fact, it is an excess of love, oblational, and asymmetrical, not seeking either correspondence or reciprocity. The love of *philia*, however, is the love of friends that is necessarily symmetrical and reciprocal. Whenever Jesus uses a word from the lexicon of love, he is teaching us something deep about it. And the narrative situations in which he makes his statements further emphasize this particular feature.

DISCIPLE AND FRIEND

Jesus had a relationship of friendship with the group of twelve disciples. This being so, who is the "disciple whom Jesus loved," described in these words only in the Gospel of John? We do not know, because he remains anonymous, an enigma preserved throughout the Gospel. His name is never given, but there are a number of references to him with details of Jesus' affection for him and these enable us to perceive that the "disciple whom Jesus loved" is a disciple who is both disciple and friend. The first time this description is used is in chapter 13 of the Gospel, in the context of the Last Supper. Jesus had just announced that one of those present would betray him. The disciples were at first astonished by this news and then curious as to who the traitor might be. "One of his disciples—the one whom Jesus loved—was reclining next to him; Simon Peter therefore motioned to him to ask Jesus of whom he was speaking. So while reclining next to Jesus, he asked him, 'Lord, who is it?'" (John 13:23–25). The beloved disciple is the one who is particularly close to Jesus, who leans on his breast, not merely in a demonstration of affection, but also of communion of life and feelings. This gesture of reclining is an image that appears in other Jewish texts and is connected with the bearing of witness. The Gospel represents, we might say, the witness of a friend; what a friend sees in Jesus concerns us deeply, putting us in his place. Thus, the beloved disciple's intervention is connected to a profound axis of the theology of John according to which it is by means of friendship that we understand Jesus and draw close to him. The beloved disciple's position within the group in no way affects Peter's position as leader. Peter is the leader of the Twelve. But on a number of occasions, Peter only manages to penetrate Jesus' secret when he makes use of the intervention of the beloved disciple (see also, for example, the episode of investigating the empty tomb, John 20:3–7).

Another highly significant moment occurred at the foot of the Cross. Standing there were his mother, his mother's sister Mary, the wife of Clopas, and Mary Magdalene. "When Jesus saw his mother and the disciple whom he loved standing beside her, he said to his mother, 'Woman, here is your son.' Then he said to the disciple, 'Here is your mother.' And from that hour the disciple took her into his own home" (John 19:26–27). There are various levels at which we can read this episode, and at this point the disciple represents the Church as a whole. But one thing is certain: there is a friendship consisting of mutual trust and intimacy between Jesus and this disciple whom he loved. One does not entrust one's mother to just anyone! Like those soldiers who are afraid that they may not survive a war and write to a special friend saying, "Look after my parents," Jesus makes this same gesture of asking the disciple whom he loved to provide the protection his mother needed.

The last time that the beloved disciple is mentioned is in John 21:24, where we read: "This is the disciple who is testifying to these things and has written them, and we know that his testimony is true." Thus, we are told that the Gospel was based on the privileged testimony of a friend. The fact that this disciple remains anonymous creates a very strong bond with the reader. The Gospel is read from the viewpoint of the beloved disciple and, symbolically, the reader shares his view of things, his attitude, and his place. The Gospel of John and friendship are, in fact, closely linked.

NOT SERVANTS, BUT FRIENDS

The Gospel of John does not describe the Last Supper in the way that the Synoptic Gospels do. However, it does include a description of how Jesus, during the supper, washed the feet of the disciples (see John 13). It is the only physical contact between them mentioned in the Gospels. The body is not extraneous to friendship, and for this reason it is so symbolic that Jesus, who is about to give his life for his friends, should wash their feet, touching each one with the radical acceptance of his friendship. In this context, Jesus utters a key text for the theology of friendship. "This is my commandment, that you love one another as I have loved you. No one has greater love than this, to lay down one's life for one's friends. You are my friends if you do what I command you. I do not call you servants any longer, because the servant does not know what the master is doing; but I have called you friends, because I have made known to you everything that I have heard from my Father" (John 15:12–15).

It may well be that, at a certain point in their relationship with Jesus, the word *servant* or even the word *disciple* was appropriate for describing what they were living. However, it is the actual following of Jesus that calls for these words to be supplanted. Now only the word *friend* is appropriate for describing someone who follows Jesus, because Jesus himself places us in a relationship of knowledge and acknowledgment of all that he has heard from his Father. Later on, the disciples' experience of friendship will be completed by the coming of the Holy Spirit who will lead them into all truth. The Spirit bears witness in their heart to all that they had not yet managed to take in: the ultimate meaning, the whole truth concerning what Jesus' friendship represents.

ARE YOU REALLY MY FRIEND?

In Jesus' last conversation with Peter, we hear the gentle lapping of the lake. It is a very striking exchange. It all turns on a subtle play of words that is not apparent in most translations. Jesus appears to ask the same question three times: "Peter, do you love me?" And gets from Peter a reply that is repeated: "You know that I love you." However, the original Greek text is much richer, as it plays on the meaning of two verbs: *philéo*, which expresses the love of friendship, and *agapáo*, which describes a total love.

Jesus begins by asking Peter: "Simon…do you love me completely?" (see John 21:15). Before the drama of the betrayal, the Apostle would have replied immediately, "Of course I love you, without any reservation." But now that he knows himself unfortunately capable of being unfaithful, he says humbly: "Lord, you know that I really am your friend." In other words, "I love you as I can, with my fragile and incomplete love." Jesus presses him a second time: "Simon, do you love me with the total love I expect from you?" And Peter stammers out a reply suited to his humble but also realistic possibilities: "Lord, you know that I am your friend." Finally, when Jesus asks the question for the third time, he uses a different form of words, saying to him this time, "So are you my friend?" Meaning, "Are you truly my friend?" Simon at last understands Jesus; that Jesus does not ask for what we are not capable of giving him. He accepts our friendship for all its weakness, our "yeses" in the making, our faltering steps. In order to enable us to reach up to him, Jesus comes down to us.

The Gospel tells us that Peter was sad because Jesus had adapted himself to our humanity. But it is this adaptation of Jesus, this radical acceptance of our poverty, his constant moving toward our friendship that is the source of our hope. As he said to the disciples at the beginning, to us too, to each one of us, Jesus simply says, "Follow me."

6

PRESENCE AS GIFT

It is a meeting out of the blue but one that epitomizes his mission, this meeting that Jesus engineers with an awkward onlooker from the tiny city of Jericho as if he were speaking to an old friend: "Zacchaeus, hurry and come down; for I must stay at your house today" (Luke 19:5). And at the end of that memorable day, Jesus further declared, to the astonishment of many, that "today salvation has come to this house" (Luke 19:9).

For the people of Jericho, Jesus was a Galilean who was believed to be a prophet, and this fact was enough to cause a large crowd of people to gather round him. They were probably unaware of the things that were being said in order to denigrate him, to the effect that he was a "friend of tax collectors and sinners" (Luke 7:34), since they too were to be critical of just this (see Luke 19:7) when, in full view of everyone, he chose to be a guest in the house of a man who was a sinner! But if we listen carefully to the conversation between Jesus and that leader of those unpopular tax collectors who has become his friend, a key feature stands out: we learn that the coming of salvation is closely linked with the experience of a friendship that overturns the limited expectations that the present seemed to offer. It was certainly not by chance that Jesus stressed the word *today*. Friendship gives a different value to time. Regardless of how modest the ways of expressing it may be, friendship with Jesus makes of time an epiphany, a place where life is gained, salvation attained.

THE "TODAY" OF FRIENDSHIP

The adverb *today* is used twelve times by Luke in his Gospel, and of these, nine are uttered directly by Jesus himself. Each one of these "todays" spoken by Jesus contains the possibility of salvation, even when, in some cases, they collide with a hardness of heart. This happens, for example, in the synagogue of his own hometown, Nazareth. Having read the messianic prophecy from the Book of Isaiah, Jesus says to those present, "Today this scripture has been fulfilled in your hearing" (Luke 4:21). But, on hearing this, instead of opening their hearts to him, they drove him out as if he were an impostor. In the same way, when Jesus sends a message to Herod saying, "Yet today, tomorrow, and the next day I must be on my way, because it is impossible for a prophet to be killed away from Jerusalem" (Luke 13:33), he knows that Herod felt he was a threat, not an opportunity. We know from our own experience: only when a friendship is sealed does the present become a place of encounter and redemption.

It is precisely this that we see in the story of Zacchaeus (see Luke 19:1–10). And there are two further occasions in the Gospel where the adverb *today* plays the same role. Both occur in extreme situations where one would say that salvation was impossible. Peter betrays Jesus' friendship, but this is not the end of the story. The memory of Jesus' words "before the cock crows *today* you will deny me three times" (see Luke 22:34, 61) becomes an essential lifeline for the reconciliation. And the robber crucified alongside Jesus starts up a friendship with him when all seems lost. Jesus murmurs to him the loveliest guarantee of his friendship: "*Today* you will be with me in Paradise" (Luke 23:43). Thus, friendship is a place where, in a mysterious way, the *today* of salvation happens.

What *today* is this? The adverb *today* also appears in St. Matthew's Gospel in the Our Father, the prayer that Jesus himself teaches us to pray. Whereas the version in St. Luke's Gospel says "give us each day our daily (*epiúsion*) bread" (Luke 11:3), the version in St. Matthew's Gospel is as follows: "Give us this day our daily (*epiúsion*) bread" (Matt 6:11). Jesus thus teaches us to ask for the gift of the present: "Give us *today*."

Our petition becomes more insistent, as it were, if we reflect on the double meaning of the Greek term, which, in the Our Father petition, we translate as "daily" or "each day." This word (*epiúsion*) can, in fact, be translated as "daily" or "each day," but it retains also another meaning, that of "imminent." We are in fact asking God for both things: for him to give us today our daily bread; and also for him to give us today the "imminent bread," "the future bread that is about to arrive." It may seem a minor detail, but it clarifies the meaning of the "today" that we live in our friendship with Jesus and with one another. Every one of our friendships is called upon to become a present that is traversed by the future of God.

LIFE IS A MYSTERY OF VISITATION

In St. Luke's Gospel, too, we find Jesus weeping over the city of Jerusalem: "As he came near and saw the city, he wept over it, saying, 'If you, even you, had only recognized on this day the things that make for peace! But now they are hidden from your eyes. Indeed, the days will come upon you, when your enemies will set up ramparts around you and surround you, and hem you in on every side. They will crush you to the ground, you and your children within you, and they will not leave within you one stone upon another; because you did not recognize the time of your visitation from God'" (19:41–44).

It is essential for us to understand life as a time of visitation. At every moment, we are being visited, and our peace of heart, the strength of our hope, depends on our ability to recognize this. Friendship is to accept that God comes to visit us through those who surround us. With our friends, we construct a history that is sacred, even though in our eyes it may seem to consist in very simple and human things. A lot depends on our being welcoming when we meet others.

There is the story of a man who, while praying, made a strange request to God: he asked him to come and visit him!

"I would like you to come to my house."

Even stranger was God's reply. God said:

"Very well. Tomorrow I will come to your house."

The man went out at once, tidied everything up, arranged everything nicely, turned things around, turned on all the lights, polished everything, opened wide the windows, and settled himself to wait at the door from early morning. Who knew quite when God might come! The man was already sitting there when, very early in the morning, a pilgrim who had been walking all night, his sandals covered in mud, began to approach:

"Don't come any nearer!"

"Please give me shelter."

"I can't."

"Why not? It's your duty to welcome a pilgrim."

"I can't. God is coming to visit my house today."

So the pilgrim went to knock at someone else's door.

Later in the morning, a little boy crept up, for he had seen some lovely apples on the table and he reached in through the window in the hope of getting hold of one. The man grabbed his arm and said:

"What are you up to?"

"Just one!"

"No, not even one! These apples are for God who is coming to visit me today."

A few hours later, the man's brother came, a brother whom he loved and who naturally wanted to stay with him as he lived a long way off. But the man sent him away, because he was expecting God that day.

The evening of that day seemed to the man the most difficult in his life. God had promised to visit him; he had waited in vain all day, since early morning! How was he going to face the night, darker than ever before? So he knelt down and poured out all his disappointment to the Lord.

"How could You make a promise and not keep it? Why did You say that You would come?"

But God replied:

"I came three times, today, and you turned me away each time."

In answer to the question, "Where does God dwell?" Martin Buber quotes the reply of a wise man that we, too, need to hear. "God dwells wherever we let Him in."

7

GOD IN THE KITCHEN

"God in the kitchen" is an intriguing way to begin, but it may serve as a prop in lighting up for us the interior of the spiritual life, this territory that is to some extent hidden away and private, like the kitchen. Everything begins with a remark made by St. Teresa of Avila in her *Book of Foundations*. It is the last book that this mystic wrote, and brings together some widely different topics compiled over the years. The general tone is that of a book of memoirs: it describes friendships and conversations, it highlights meetings and disagreements, records dates, shares secrets, and so on. In a certain way, it is perhaps one of the books that best reflects the humanity of Teresa of Jesus, her delight in telling stories, well-seasoned with humor and with an extraordinary capacity to penetrate the heart.

In chapter 5, we find the following story:

> Someone I was talking to a few days ago. For about fifteen years his obedience had laid on him such hard work in offices and the oversight of others that in the whole of that time he could not remember that he had had one day to himself....The Lord has well rewarded him: for, without knowing how, he finds himself to have gained that liberty of spirit, so greatly prized and desired, which is possessed by the perfect wherein lies all the felicity that can be desired in this life....That person is not the only one I have known: for there have been others like him

whom I had not seen for many years; and when I asked them how these years had been spent, it was all in works of obedience and charity, and on the other hand I could see that they had made marvelous progress in spiritual things. Well then, my daughters! Let there be no repining when obedience keeps you employed in exterior works. Remember that even if it is in the kitchen, the Lord walks among the pots and pans. (7–8)

Saint Teresa alludes to this meeting with some of her friends who were leading a very active life, immersed in a multiplicity of projects and commitments, and who, nonetheless, had attained a spiritual vitality. There is, in fact, a centuries-old misunderstanding that, within our own perception of things, sees a dichotomy between action and contemplation. It is as if the active life necessarily drives us out into a kind of desert, propelling us far from ourselves and from God. At this point, in addressing her contemplative sisters, Saint Teresa criticizes this false view of things and tells them that outward activities need not separate us from the deepest spiritual experience. Even the most ordinary or smallest exterior gesture, even the trivial routine gestures such as those that are part of the kitchen routine (and can we really say they are trivial?) must be viewed differently, because Almighty God, the great Lord of the Universe, is there present in our kitchen, in amongst the mugs, the saucepans, the buckets, the casseroles, and other dishes.

I like a comment made by the philosopher Paul Ricoeur who says: "Without a translation, the phrases of the entire world would disappear among men like inaccessible butterflies." Unless we accept the risk of translating and making concrete, the reality of God who comes to meet us becomes fleeting and intangible. We may smile when we read St. Teresa, and this is already something. But it would be a pity if our initial reaction of delight did not help us to feel called to open up new meanings and perceive the hope they offer us.

ENTERING THE MOST HIDDEN ROOM

To say that God is moving about in the kitchen, that he is actually in among the pots and pans, implies locating the relationship with God and our acknowledgment of his presence in a context of proximity. It is a proximity that is so close that it makes us feel somewhat embarrassed. But God in the kitchen? Why there and not in the drawing room or the dining room? There is a closeness that makes us feel a kind of bashfulness, or indeed a sense of shock or even fear. We prefer to deal with the question of God in a neutral context. And in his neutrality, God is invisible. He is transcendent, odorless, harmless, tasteless—God calms us down. The proximity that the metaphor of the kitchen suggests disturbs because it seems that God is going to enter a space that is not fitting for him and, deep down, we still feel that there are places that are suitable for God and others that are not.

In addition to this conflict between proximity and neutrality, there is another, that between the representation and the reality. It is not that we are actors or that we are not quite straightforward in the way we relate to God, but the expression of our spirituality does include much representation. It is liturgical gestures and rites that underlie our prayer, for example. We repeat words that are not our own and are very different from those that we normally use. There is a whole memory that we mime and repeat in order to say God and express ourselves to him. And very often we find that the spiritual life consists in this heritage of practices that we have inherited, which we repeat, and copy, and transmit. There are times when, between the space of representation, which is also both necessary and precious, and the space of our own reality, there develops a lack of symmetry, a tangle of misunderstandings.

INNER SPACE DICHOTOMIES

Our houses are enclosed spaces that are divided up into sections. This explains why we find so strange the so-called *open-space* schemes that so many organizations are fond of nowadays. We need marked-off spaces: the drawing room is one thing, the bedroom another, the kitchen another. Many writers, for example, have explored the dichotomies that there can be between the dining room and the kitchen. The dining room is the place for conviviality, order, the rules of etiquette, of a faultless, ornamental, and perfect refinement, as if on a stage. And the kitchen is the other side, the technicians and scene shifters who are perhaps closer to reality, but also far from perfect, untidy, with stains, saucepans put down anywhere, with little attention paid to appearances. The dining room is a place of enjoyment, as it were, a pleasant interval in which to enjoy a break, and the kitchen is a symbol of servile work, enforced and unappreciated. We have grown accustomed to thinking of our spiritual life as a performance, a show that is put on in the drawing room where we appear dressed in order to see God inside and out. We have a feeling that our trivial and routine day-to-day lives are not for God; we do not feel they are on the level of the sacred. Nevertheless, St. Teresa tells us, "God walks among the pots and pans."

It is interesting to see how Jesus dealt with this performance/reality dualism. In chapter 6 of Matthew's Gospel, he says, "And whenever you pray, do not be like the hypocrites; for they love to stand and pray in the synagogues and at street corners, so that they may be seen by others. Truly I tell you, they have received their reward. But whenever you pray, go into your room and shut the door and pray to your Father who is in secret" (6:5–6). We have here the flight from and relativization of all performance. Obviously, it is a good thing to pray in the synagogue, as Jesus himself did. But the reality of our prayer cannot be restricted to this context, leaving uninhabited our "own hidden room." Spiritual expressions can be dangerous if they do no more than keep up an appearance and are empty of our own uniqueness and of God's real transcendence. To enter into the innermost room in our house is the guarantee that the performance has been relativized and that in the hidden place, in the place where we are most ourselves, we are seeking a personal, humble, and true relationship with God. We are living his friendship.

THINKING OF GOD STARTING FROM THE RAW AND THE COOKED

Let us reflect on the question of God on the basis of the raw and the cooked. *The Raw and the Cooked* is a work by the anthropologist Claude Lévi-Strauss in which he studies various native myths from the Amazon in which the common factor is an explanation of the use of fire in the kitchen.

Why pay particular attention to Lévi-Strauss on this account? Because, according to him, the kitchen is the place that marks the transition from nature to culture. The raw represents the natural state of things. The cooked represents transformation brought about by human beings. The kitchen represents the construction of man's autonomy in relation to nature, his capacity to be different and to be. Human beings are not merely the fruit of natural circumstances; they also contribute something of themselves, something unique.

In the majority of these myths, the appearance of fire and of cooking comes about at the cost of a break with the divinity. This is described in the mythological tale of Prometheus, who stole fire from the gods in order to give it to human beings; for this he suffered a harsh punishment. Cooking, therefore, is presented as a break with the Divine, a concentration on human beings and their possibilities. Hence, St.

Teresa's image of God who is in the kitchen has more implications than a preliminary reading might at first seem to suggest. God goes to the kitchen and does not criticize human beings for their independence. There is no competition: God does not reprimand them for creating a space that is different from that of nature, of creation. God appears as the One who inspires. The image suggested by St. Teresa comes as a surprise, but is also pacifying: "Even in the kitchen, the Lord walks among the pots and pans."

With Claude Lévi-Strauss, we also learn that the kitchen is above all the place of transformation, as distinct from nature, which presents us with lines of unchanging continuity. So many transformations take place in each of our kitchens that they are almost invisible and they already seem to us quite banal. The kitchen is the place of instability, of the search for things, of uncertainty, of unexpected mixtures, of unforeseen solutions, of altered recipes. The kitchen is the place for creativity and for recomposition. For this reason, it is often untidy when it ought not to be, because the function of the kitchen is to live in this underlying state of recomposition. The anthropologist teaches us that cooking is a metaphor for human existence itself, as it distinguishes the human being, precisely in this capacity of living in a state of transformation, in a mobility that is not solely geographical.

St. Teresa's words become increasingly complex when we think about what a kitchen is. It is very easy to identify ourselves in relation to God with set lines. The great paradigms that we have inherited speak of the spiritual life on the basis of continuity and repetition. The ideal would be to remain always the same, unaltered. But the metaphor of the kitchen speaks of transformation as a benefit. Very often, our conflict and our anguish are born of this impasse: on the one hand, we are not capable of maintaining the lines of continuity that we are aiming for and on the other, we are not really ready to value the modifications that we constantly experience from the spiritual point of view.

GOD IS VISIBLE, WE ARE INVISIBLE

The philosopher and anthropologist Michel de Certeau, with a team of investigators, paid great attention to the anthropology of everyday life and to a survey of its signs, seeing in this, which is looked upon as secondary or nonhistory, significant forms for understanding the human *habitat*. Each one of us, if questioned about our lives, would concentrate on a series of dates that highlight the great events, the extraordinary. However, what shapes our lives more forcibly is this silent and unseen dimension that the paradigm of the kitchen helps to reveal. This life in spaces that are not public, not publishable, as is the image of each one of us in his or her kitchen, manifests life in all its concreteness, in its toil, its difficulties, and its desires. This is because the kitchen is also the place for wishing. And the kitchen has been connected with desire ever since we were tiny babies seeking our mother's milk. This connection is with us always.

I love the way de Certeau described his project: "It is everyday life that reveals us most intimately....It is a semi-history of ourselves, almost a portrait, though sometimes veiled; we must not forget this 'world memory' to use Péguy's expression. We are attached to this world by our heart, our olfactory memory, our memory of places in our childhood, our memory of the body, of gestures, pleasures....What interests the historian of everyday life is what is invisible."

AN EVERYDAY MYSTICISM

To speak of the kitchen is to speak of our own invisibility. How are we to assess the value of this dimension through which God passes? Or rather: how do we allow ourselves to be traversed by God in our invisibility? It is very convenient to say that God is invisible and we ourselves are visible. But behind one truth, there is always another. This other truth whispers to us that God is visible, and we ourselves are invisible. The kitchen calls to mind this ingredient, conceivably the most intimate and original, that constitutes us and is connected with our body, our desire, our battle to survive, our pleasures: the encounter in which the transformations that we bring about in things also reflect that which takes place within ourselves. It is a tremendous challenge to move from a spirituality that is based on the experience of the extraordinary to one of everyday life, to a spirituality capable of taking in the dimensions of this invisible memory that each one of us possesses.

I remember a Zen story that tells of a disciple who is about to be assessed by the master. For seven years, he had learned, listened, sought with admirable patience, looked into the great books, and sat in silence before the wise authorities. He was now about to enter the room where the master would ask him a question, just one question, but one that would decide everything. Would he know how to reply, and, if so, would he himself become a master? During the final few days, the disciple applied himself even more assiduously to his studies. There was nothing that one can know about the sky, the earth, or the depths that he, in fact, did not know. When he appeared before the master, however, the interrogation could not have been more disconcerting. The master merely asked him, "When you came into the room, where did you leave your shoes? To the right or the left of the cupboard?"

GIVING AND RECEIVING

Did Jesus go to the kitchen? Did he speak and think of the kitchen as the place for this invisible, unsayable, transforming memory that each man and woman carries within them? Eating and drinking are very important as a means of understanding all religions and all human groups. Anthropologists say that when we know where people eat, how they eat, with whom they eat, and what they eat, we know the most important things about them. Christianity, too, took great interest in food but, unlike the other two monotheist religions, Judaism and Islamism, it did away with dietary prohibitions. The table and meal have become, above all, the place of memorial, of encounter and of Christian utopia.

Jesus did not teach us to cook a particular dish. Reading the Gospels will not equip us to prepare a meal, but we shall be capable of organizing a banquet: who the priority guests are to be, where we are to sit, what our attitude is to be, and so on. He was accused by his enemies of being a glutton and a drunkard, and this might seem to be true. One of the last things he said was: "I have eagerly desired to eat this Passover with you" (Luke 22:15). Eating was not a mere routine in the life of Jesus. It is interesting that the verb he used was *desired*, because a meal is linked to desire.

The Gospels describe a number of meals for us, the meaning of which we weaken if we read them principally from the point of view of the miracle and the marvelous, which leaves us alert but not disturbed. We can very quickly grow accustomed to miracles. We forget that meals are the performative acts of Jesus in which he explains the unusualness of his project, assembling round the same table those who cannot normally be brought together, spreading out in a fraternal and egalitarian field a countless multitude of men and women.

But, in addition to the meals, there are at least two episodes in which Jesus looks beyond the table and his gaze extends as far as the kitchen. The first of these episodes is the story of his friends Martha and Mary (Luke 10:38–42).

> Now as they went on their way, he entered a certain village, where a woman named Martha welcomed him into her home. She had a sister named Mary, who sat at the Lord's feet and listened to what he was saying. But Martha was distracted by her many tasks; so she came to him and asked, "Lord, do you not care that my sister has left me to do all the work by myself? Tell her then to help me." But the Lord

answered her, "Martha, Martha, you are worried and distracted by many things; there is need of only one thing. Mary has chosen the better part, which will not be taken away from her."

Jesus looks critically at the way Martha is living her existence in the kitchen. The Gospel narrator, who is normally very precise, describes this as being "distracted by her many tasks" and at a distance from the guest. When she seeks to involve her sister, too, in this service, Jesus criticizes this way of doing things that leaves no room for the one thing necessary: receiving the gift, being aware of the gift, the gift of that guest. There is a way of doing things that is in dialogue with the gift, but there is also another way that makes us forget the meaning and the savor of the gift. There is a way of doing things that is only doing things, and there is another that makes us more receptive—not to be concerned merely about giving, but also to be attuned to the gift. The kitchen may be no more than a place in which to do things, to be of service, to provide for needs routinely, rather than a place of discovery. Jesus wants Martha to find herself in the middle of her kitchen. The relationship between having to give, having to serve, and actually giving and serving is not always clear.

AT DAWN WHEN JESUS COOKED

The other episode occurs in chapter 21 of the Gospel of St. John and describes Jesus' last meal.

> After these things Jesus showed himself again to the disciples by the Sea of Tiberias; and he showed himself in this way. Gathered there together were Simon Peter, Thomas called the Twin, Nathanael of Cana in Galilee, the sons of Zebedee, and two others of his disciples. Simon Peter said to them, "I am going fishing." They said to him, "We will go with

you." They went out and got into the boat, but that night they caught nothing.

Just after daybreak, Jesus stood on the beach; but the disciples did not know that it was Jesus. Jesus said to them, "Children, you have no fish, have you?" They answered him, "No." He said to them, "Cast the net to the right side of the boat, and you will find some." So they cast it, and now they were not able to haul it in because there were so many fish. That disciple whom Jesus loved said to Peter, "It is the Lord!" When Simon Peter heard that it was the Lord, he put on some clothes, for he was naked, and jumped into the lake. But the other disciples came in the boat, dragging the net full of fish, for they were not far from the land, only about a hundred yards off.

When they had gone ashore, they saw a charcoal fire there, with fish on it, and bread. Jesus said to them, "Bring some of the fish that you have just caught." So Simon Peter went aboard and hauled the net ashore, full of large fish, a hundred fifty-three of them; and though there were so many, the net was not torn. Jesus said to them, "Come and have breakfast." Now none of the disciples dared to ask him, "Who are you?" because they knew it was the Lord. Jesus came and took the bread and gave it to them, and did the same with the fish. This was now the third time that Jesus appeared to the disciples after he was raised from the dead. (John 21:1–14)

This episode is very interesting because of the intermingling of two stories: the story of fruitless toil that Jesus transformed into abundance, and the more silent story within this one, the story of a friend who, at the cusp between night and dawn of those difficult days of growth that were the days of

Passover, prepares fish and bread to offer his friends. It is important that the toil, the work, the need to bring in those one hundred and fifty-three large fish, not stand in the way of the sense of wonder and the desire to receive. There, the important thing is not what they thought, but the single fish that Jesus had placed on the fire in that early dawn. It is important that the routine of cooking does not diminish the dynamism of the gift, for us to be ourselves gifts accepting gifts one from another.

FROM THE ORNAMENTAL TO THE REAL: RECOVERING THE THREAD OF DESIRE

There is a very challenging text by Roland Barthes that is included in his work *Mythologies*, entitled "Ornamental Cookery." It is an analysis of something that appears to be quite frivolous. Glossy magazines pay great attention to cooking, but to a kind of cooking that one cannot actually do, as it is so very exquisite, so baroque and extreme that it can really only be looked at with the eyes, as it appears on paper. It is a question of a kind of food that is mythological, unreproducible, ornamental. He writes:

> The weekly *Elle* gives us almost every week a fine coloured photograph of a prepared dish: golden partridges studded with cherries, a faintly pink chicken chaud-froid, a mould of crayfish surrounded by their red shells, a frothy charlotte prettified with frosted fruit designs, multi-coloured trifle, etc....Ornamentation proceeds in two contradictory ways: on the one hand fleeing from nature, thanks to a kind of frenzied baroque (sticking shrimps in a lemon, making a chicken look pink, serving grapefruit hot) and, on the other, trying to

reconstitute it through an incongruous artifice (strewing meringues, mushrooms and holly leaves on a traditional log-shaped Christmas cake, replacing the heads of crayfish around the sophisticated béchamel which hides their bodies)....Cookery in *Elle* is an "idea" cookery. But here inventiveness, confined to a fairy-land reality, must be applied only to *garnishing*, for the genteel tendency of the magazine precludes it from touching on the real problems concerning food.

There is also a spiritual life made entirely of paper, with seasonal resolutions for garnishing in which we have to insert cherries into lemons and frenziedly decorate our inner journey. To what extent can our spirituality escape the ornamental? We may well find the solution by returning to our kitchen and there recognizing that God is present in this real place. And, in the truest depth of ourselves, he allows us to recover the thread of friendship and desire.

8

AT TABLE WE TASTE THE FRIENDSHIP OF JESUS

It is true that the Eucharist (see Luke 22:19–20), which is the center of the life of the Kingdom, is a meal, and that it concentrates around a table the entire destiny of Jesus, as if all his gestures and words finally flowed together into the unity of a single gesture and a single word. But the Eucharist itself began as a nontypical meal, filled with a semantics irreducible to this framework. From the beginning, it was described and received, in the faith of the Christian community, as the radical Gift of himself that Jesus made and as a fellowship that gathers the believers around this event. Nevertheless, what becomes clear is that, in addition to the Eucharist, the Gospels are bound together by the memory of other meals. And these, by placing Jesus in a symbolic position full of implications, bring out for us the deep meaning of the friendship of Jesus.

THE ANTHROPOLOGICAL SIGNIFICANCE OF "EATING TOGETHER"

To eat with others is to transform the satisfying of a primary need into a social moment of far-reaching importance. The table reflects life as in a mirror. What happens at table is not merely the fulfillment of a biological need, but the significant expression of some of the codes that are intrinsic to a culture. In Plutarch, we read that one does not sit down at table simply in order to eat, but in order to eat *with* and, in the context of the values of the Mediterranean world of that time, this conviviality distinguished civilized people from barbarians.

Company at table makes the need for food a kind of microcosm that reflects desires and prohibitions, customs, and exchanges of meaning. As we observe the way in which meals are taken, we gain an interior structure, values, and hierarchies of a specific human group, as well as the limits that it imposes on the world around it. For, when one comes to perceive the logic and the content of the food that is being eaten, as well as the order that governs the meal (with whom one eats, how one eats, the logic of the various places and functions at table, and so on), one acquires some very important knowledge.

Just look at Greek banquets. They took place normally in two stages: the meal itself, properly speaking, and the symposium, a time after the meal devoted to drinking and to conversation. This was the moment at which the theme of the general conversation in which all the guests were interested emerged. The table is also a language pact, because the guests bring as a gift the narration of their history. It is a space and time when, in telling one's story, one comes to terms with oneself. Surrounded by those who are listening to me, I am given an opportunity to speak of myself, to put the pieces back together, to re-tie broken laces, to find the words that conceal the intimate architecture of life. We can recall the example of Ulysses, who, during the various stages of his return to Ithaca, assumes the role of guest and gradually reveals his identity. At a certain point, for example, the king of the Phaeacians asked him: "My guest, do not conceal from me…what I am going to ask you; speak openly! Tell me what, in your own country, your father and mother and the other occupants of the city call you.…Give me, too, the name of your homeland, your people and your native city."

Very quickly, the symposium (insofar as it is both a reality and a literary device) also becomes a privileged territory for the practice of philosophy. In Plato and Xenophon, Socrates is the principal guest at the feasts, and the purpose of the symposium extends beyond the narrow framework of a meal and turns into a disputed search for truth.

A BIBLICAL IDEAL

Even today, it is said that "one learns Judaism by eating." Beginning with what is written in the Law (Lev 11; Deut 14) and in the tradition, we can say that the choices of food made by a member of the people of God form the basis of their identity. In fact, we should not forget that the first commandment that God gave to Adam and Eve, in the story of the garden, concerned food ("You may freely eat of every tree of the garden; but of the tree of the knowledge of good and evil you shall not eat, for in the day that you eat of it you shall die" [Gen 2:16–17]); that the promised land is above all defined in terms of food and drink, a land "flowing with milk and honey" (Deut 6:3; 8:8; 11:9; 26:9–10, 15; 27:3; 31:20; 32:13–14); that the purpose of Moses' long trek with the people from the Red Sea to the river Jordan was to eat and rejoice before the LORD (Deut 27:7). The Exodus concludes with an idealization of a communal banquet: a banquet celebrated in the abundance of the fruits of the earth and in the solidarity among all the members of the people.

Later, in the prophetic literature, the paradigm of the banquet becomes a theme that proclaims the messianic times. The implicit presence of the Messiah causes the fullness of God's salvation to break into the shipwrecks and disasters of history. This messianic re-creation is frequently represented by the image of a banquet: "On this mountain the LORD of hosts will make for all peoples a feast of rich food, a feast of well-matured wines….Then the LORD God will wipe away the tears from all faces" (Isa 25:6, 8). And the poor are not excluded from this banquet: "Everyone who thirsts, come to the waters; and you that have no money, come, buy and eat! Come, buy wine and milk without money and without price" (Isa 55:1); and to them especially is repeated the promise of new times: "Eat what is good and delight yourselves in rich food" (Isa 55:2).

At the practical level, however, this biblical ideal did not often move beyond precisely this, an ideal. For the reality is that table fellowship served to reinforce lines of division, consolidating mechanisms of exclusion in both the social and religious fabric. Against this, we have the prophecy of Amos condemning "those who lie on beds of ivory, and lounge on their couches, and eat lambs from the flock, and calves from the stall; who sing idle songs to the sound of the harp, and like David improvise on instruments of music; who drink wine from bowls and anoint themselves with the finest oils, but are not grieved over the ruin of Joseph!" (Amos 6:4–6).

JESUS, GUEST OF THE PHARISEES

One of the special features of St. Luke's Gospel is that he three times tells us that Jesus was invited to dine with the Pharisees: "One of the Pharisees asked Jesus to eat with him" (Luke 7:36); "While he was speaking, a Pharisee invited him to dine with him" (Luke 11:37); "On one occasion when Jesus was going to the house of a leader of the Pharisees to eat a meal on the sabbath" (Luke 14:1). Although, in themselves, these occasions constitute undeniable evidence of a liking for Jesus on the part of the Pharisees (which even makes us think that the third Gospel to some extent tones down the anti-Pharisee tone of the other Synoptics), they do not cease to be episodes dominated by controversy, for Jesus proves to be an awkward guest. In the first of these meals (7:36–50), Jesus allows a woman who is a sinner to touch him, thereby contaminating that situation with impurity, and, on seeing this, his Pharisee host began to wonder whether or not he was a prophet. In the second episode, in connection with the custom of ritual ablutions, Jesus utters a violent condemnation of the ritualistic hypocrisy of the Pharisees and scribes who cleanse the outside of things while the inside remains full of "greed and wickedness" (11:39). This speech gives rise to their persecution of Jesus (11:53). During the third meal, Jesus heals a man suffering from dropsy on a Sabbath and criticizes their table etiquette (the choice of guests and the strategy of where they are seated), concluding with the parable of the rejected banquet at which the guests were to be those deemed the least appropriate (the poor and maimed and blind and lame).

The banquets with the Pharisees represent, in Jesus' way, an experience of confrontation rather than of encounter, because Jesus and his mission could not be absorbed into that religiosity based on exclusion. What we see is the exclusive pharisaic milieu being invaded by sinners seeking out Jesus and being welcomed by him. The issue will be Jesus' friendship with them. The problem was not, strictly speaking, the fact that Jesus ate and drank, because John the Baptist's asceticism, too, had been firmly rejected by the authorities (see Luke 7:33). The issue was that Jesus ate and drank in the company of sinners, turning table fellowship into a place of meeting beyond the frontiers established by the Law. And Jesus brings into the parable of those who refuse the eschatological banquet, precisely those who were regarded as outcasts. The poor, the impure, and pagans, exactly those types that good people were obliged to keep away from their table, are more than invited, they are impelled, obliged, to come to the banquet, thereby expressing the triumph of grace over their lack of preparation (see Luke 14:15–24). How are we to understand this friendship of Jesus?

JESUS, FRIEND OF SINNERS

By accepting to eat with sinners, Jesus was violating the powerful system of purity. But the truth is that Jesus' gesture is not merely one of rupture, but the affirmation of a new experience of God. In the line of the universalist interpretation of the messianic banquet foretold for the future by the prophets, Jesus was claiming for his "today" a religious way of life that went beyond the bounds of legality, by bringing those who had been excluded back to friendship with God.

Jesus' intention can be deduced from the first meal that he ate with sinners in the home of the tax collector Levi. After Jesus had called him to be a disciple, Levi gave a banquet. Now the Pharisees and scribes criticized the fact that Jesus and his disciples were mixing with people regarded as impure: "Why do you eat and drink with tax collectors and sinners?" (Luke 5:30). The reply that Jesus gave constitutes a kind of key for reading the originality of his ministry. In fact, Jesus was not endeavoring to bring about the abolition of the norms to which they were so attached, but spoke of the emergence of a greater need: "Those who are well have no need of a physician, but those who are sick" (Luke 5:31).

There is a sapiential, almost explanatory, note in this statement in which Jesus compares himself to the doctor who runs the risk of contagion in order to perform his duty to care for the sick. Jesus has come to call sinners to conversion. He does not look at sinners in the abstract, or in an attitude of making excuses, but seeing each one integrated in the concrete historic situations that serve as a point of departure for a true friendship, which is always a transforming experience.

Without the slightest hesitation, Jesus turns his attention to those regarded as impure because of illness, possession, or a blemish of some kind. Contrary to the regulation contained in Leviticus 21:17–20, he declared that the maimed, the lame, and the blind were to be the privileged guests at the banquet (Luke 14:12–14). He kept up an acknowledged table fellowship with morally unacceptable people. He was seen with sinners and tax collectors and he sat down with them at table. And he did not protect himself, nor did he display any dislike of being touched by a public sinner (Luke 7:37–39).

It is curious to note how subtly the evangelist contradicts

and dismantles this image of Jesus as he tells the story. Jesus states in Luke 5:32: "I have come to call not the righteous but sinners to repentance." The typically Lucan addition "to repentance" makes it very clear that, underlying the whole way of describing the particular person, is the radical transformation of situations. Luke, for example, never tires of emphasizing this: the dead whom Jesus touches are brought back to life; the woman with an issue of blood is healed; the blind begin to see; the sinner has her sins forgiven. Jesus established a relationship between people and God, relativizing or giving a new meaning to the purity laws. Everything is connected with Jesus' own attitude to God and his personal identity.

For the Pharisees and scribes, Jesus went much too far in his table fellowship by sitting down at the same table with sinners, since such table fellowship established a link between them. They did not want to see the extent to which Jesus' friendship provided the opportunity for a radical conversion that was inaugurating the time of the Kingdom of God in those particular lives. It is certain that the experiences of mercy and of God's forgiveness are not, strictly speaking, a novelty relative to the earlier biblical tradition. But this insistence, prefigured in friendship, of a gift of unconditional and immediate divine mercy (it is not the sinners who are converted in order to obtain mercy; the sinners receive mercy and so are converted!), is so unusual that it appears to be scandalous. For it is not only the symbolic act that Jesus will perform later, that of the purification of the temple (Luke 19:45–46) and prophecy of the destruction of the temple itself (Luke 21:5–7) that bring him into collision with the priestly authorities. It is his own ministry proclaiming a new autonomy in relation to the supervision that the temple provided over the religiosity of Israel. By being seen, in friendly table fellowship with sinners, as "the one who forgives sins," Jesus was claiming to have made the temple obsolete. In a way, the temple rites had lost their effectiveness. Only those who encountered Jesus were touched by a faith that saves (Luke 17:19).

BARRIERS TO HAPPINESS

But Jesus does far more than proclaim that he has come for sinners. His declaration extends further, and is both more polemical and more decisive: "Those who are well have no need of a physician, but those who are sick; I have come to call not the righteous but sinners to repentance" (Luke 5:31–32). Could it be that in saying this Jesus was setting aside the righteous so that he too, in his turn, is excluding people? What Jesus does is to state that sinners are aware of their lack of contact and friendship, as they realize their "need of a physician," whereas those who regard themselves as righteous, enclose themselves in a human fiction about themselves. The awareness of a personal or group righteousness works like a barrier, making it difficult or impossible to recognize the novelty that Jesus promises. Hence, the model for the attitude to Jesus that the gospel narrative recommends is that of the sinner. The first thing that even Peter, the leader of the disciples, says to Jesus is: "Go away from me, Lord, for I am a sinful man!" (Luke 5:8). His recognition of his own fragility worked as a way of making him open to the friendship of Jesus.

Chapter 15 of the Gospel of St. Luke, the so-called gospel of lost things (the sheep, the drachma, the son), takes off from an accusation against Jesus. The first verses (1–2) present us with the following picture: "Now all the tax collectors and sinners were coming near to listen to him. And the Pharisees and the scribes were grumbling and saying, 'This fellow welcomes sinners and eats with them.'" Jesus' reply (the three parables of mercy) did not console the ears of his audience.

The description in the third of the parables (Luke 15:11–32), of the behavior of a father who, instead of heaping well-deserved reproaches on his returning errant son, orders a banquet to celebrate his return—a banquet such as he had never organized for his elder son who had remained at his side—breaks with the acceptable idea of God. Not only was Jesus revealing a God who runs to embrace the return of the prodigal, but a God whom we can lose if we do not accept him as he is in his boundless yearning for friendship.

God urges the righteous person to celebrate with joy the conversion of the sinner: "Rejoice with me, for I have found my sheep that was lost" (Luke 15:6); "Rejoice with me, for I have found the coin that I had lost" (Luke 15:9); "But we had to celebrate and rejoice, because…he was lost and has been found" (Luke 15:32). The loyalty of the older brother, that fidelity of which he himself reminds his father ("Listen! For all these years I have been working like a slave for you, and I have never disobeyed your command" [Luke 15:29]) and which the father acknowledges ("Son, you are always with me" [Luke 15:31]), would be his greatest trial in accepting the return of his brother. The joy of conversion is only complete if the righteous one genuinely welcomes home the lost brother, and takes his place at the feast in that house from which are heard, St. Luke tells us, "music and dancing" (Luke 15:25).

Table fellowship and friendship with sinners could be regarded, by those who were against it, as an act of insolence on the part of Jesus, a kind of anarchy from the social and religious point of view. But it was much more than this: it was a statement that, with himself, the kingdom had come, and that universal and unfettered joy was really possible. It is no wonder that friendship becomes a fundamental feature of the christological revelation.

9

A FRIEND IS A WITNESS

We are made of time; we are kneaded from the clay of time; we are made of ages, seasons, hours, days: we are made of timepieces, that is, of the means of measuring time, visible and invisible. In fact, everything that is human is made of time: we are a reservoir of time, sheets of time that are gradually accumulating. To say all this in one word: we are *duration*.

Very often, when we come to look at our face, we realize with surprise that time has passed. We experience two situations: we are either acutely aware of the passage of time, or else time is a surprise for us, as we do not realize that it has passed, or that it has passed in this way. In a fervent spiritual life, we need to meditate on time. There is a passage in a work by Romano Guardini entitled *Die Annahme seiner selbst* (*The acceptance of oneself*) that seems to me very relevant from this point of view. He writes, "For myself, I am not simply something obvious. I am also something strange, enigmatic; I could even say that I am a stranger."

To speak of time is to speak of this complex apparition to ourselves, to refer to our surprise, acknowledge our astonishment at being, at times, complete strangers to ourselves. When I look at myself, whom do I see? When I look at myself, is it myself that I see? I now perceive that this person whom I thought I knew very well, with an unquestionable stability—I am this, I am that—is now mutating, as each one of us is a flux, a journey, an open-ended project, an incomplete manifestation. St. Augustine wrote in his *Confessions*: "What then is time? If no one asks me, I know what it is. If I wish to explain to the one who asks, I do not know" (Book XI).

A FRIEND IS A WITNESS

A proverb says, "To live without friends is to die without witnesses." Friends attest to our lives. They know what time is for us. They bear witness to the fact that we are, that we have done things, that we love, that we pursue particular dreams, and that we were pursued by this or that form of suffering. And they do all this without the superficiality that, most of the time, is conventional, in the committed way of someone who is a genuine companion. The gaze of a friend is an anchor. We cling to it at different stages of our lives in order to receive the priceless gift that we absolutely need and that, in truth, only friendship can give us: the certainty that we are being accompanied and are acknowledged. Without this, life is an underlying blur destined to be forgotten.

Each one of us lives his or her story through the need for recognition. For there to be an "I," there has to be a "you." With every child that is born into the world, there is born also something that had never previously existed, something new and unique, but it is in the construction of reciprocity that we can discover it consistently. The "I" has an imperious need to be regarded favorably by the other and by others in order to organize itself and run the risk of being. Even Aristotle, in his *Nicomachean Ethics* wrote: "A happy man needs friends." We become ill in the absence of friends. We need this mutual, person-to-person, recognition: a recognition not based on comparison or competition, but on affection; not determined merely by the laws of justice or the bonds of blood, but rooted in gratuitousness.

Filled with a wisdom very much steeped in the Bible, Martin Buber reminds us that in order to be human, life cannot be restricted merely to the sphere of transitive verbs: what I do, what I buy, what I eat, and so on. Transitive verbs belong to the realm of the "It." But the truth is that the "It" is not enough; we need a "Thou." The "It" is a thing that we possess. On the other hand, anyone who says "Thou" possesses no thing and, strictly speaking, possesses nothing: he or she remains simply in relation. And relation is our beginning.

YOU WILL BE MY WITNESSES

It is no accident that Jesus hoped each disciple would become one of his witnesses. The entire journey that occupied by far the greatest part of the gospel narratives consisted not so much in a period of intellectual formation as in a school of friendship and life. "'Rabbi' (which translated means Teacher), 'where are you staying?' He said to them, 'Come and see.' They came and saw where he was staying, and they remained with him that day" (John 1:38–39). "To stay with," "to remain," "to walk alongside" are all synonyms of the word *friendship*.

Friendship is not fed on occasional meetings or on extraordinary events. Friendship is ongoing. It has the flavor of day-to-day life, of domestic situations, of meals shared, of uneventful hours, of intimacy, leisured conversations, time spent narrating details, laughter and tears, the sharing of confidences, what happened in the course of a journey or a day spent fishing. Friendship has the flavor of hospitality, of busy times, of time spent listening. Friendship fills the house with fragrance (see John 12:3). Friendship is the space for phrases like "Have you anything to eat?" (John 21:5); "What were you arguing about on the way?" (Mark 9:33); "Come…and rest for a while" (Mark 6:31); "Let us go across to the other side" (Mark 4:35). Friendship is not satisfied with the public account of events, but always seeks to view things differently, from a different angle, in order to see more deeply. In this sense, the Gospel itself tells us that Jesus spoke in parables to the crowds, but then took the disciples aside in order to explain to them the meaning of his message (Mark 4:33–34). The disciples can be appointed as witnesses because they lived a history of friendship of which they are the bearers. Here too we can apply the lesson that the fox taught to the little prince in Saint-Exupéry's book: "It was the time you spent with your rose that made your rose so important to you." There is a quality of relationship that can only come with time shared. Only with time do we discover the meaning and the relevance of our walking side by side. Without this, we become strangers to one another. "I do not call you servants any longer, because the servant does not know what the master is doing; but I have called you friends, because I have made known to you everything that I have heard from my Father" (John 15:15).

It is pertinent to note that, in the early Church, the right to proclaim the Gospels was directly linked to the fact of having been a witness (and in this sense also a friend). Truly precious are the words that form the prologue to the first Letter of John:

> We declare to you what was from the beginning, what we have heard, what we have seen with our eyes, what we have looked at and touched with our hands, concerning the word of life—this life was revealed, and we have seen it and testify to it, and declare to you the eternal life that was with the Father and was revealed to us—we declare to you what we have seen and heard so that you also may have fellowship with us; and truly our fellowship is with the Father and with his Son Jesus Christ. (1:1–3)

BEING A CHRISTIAN TODAY

According to the theologian Karl Rahner, "the Church has been led by the Lord of history into a new age." I feel no one will remain indifferent to the truth of this statement when we look at the extent of the changes that are taking place today in the religious field. It is not merely a question of the drastic reduction in numbers when one compares today's statistics with what the figures once were for the practice of the faith. The question is much more complex. It may be that what we are discovering today, even in the midst of upheavals and uncertainties, is a different way of being a believer, expressed in different forms in its needs, searching, and ways of belonging. We are not witnessing the gradual disappearance of Christianity, as is claimed by some who are too eager to describe our societies as post–Christian. Anyone who does not realize that the radical place of Christianity was always there in the midst of change does not really grasp its essence. There are, however, pointers that are becoming sufficiently clear so that it is increasingly our duty to proclaim them and take them into account.

I will mention three such pointers: first, Christians are once again becoming a "little flock." With the disappearance of a Christianity that was handed on from generation to generation as an unquestioned inheritance within more homogeneous social mechanisms, Christians are once again becoming so by personal choice, a choice often made against the tide, and reached in isolation in relation to the immediate circles to which one belongs. Whether or not we become Christians is no longer something that can be taken for granted. This happens, and happens increasingly frequently, as an option and a surprise.

Second, to the degree to which we are witnessing a weakening of official membership of the churches, we are rediscovering the value and the possibilities of a discreet presence in the midst of the world. In very many situations, in this cultural diaspora in which we find ourselves, the only acceptable word is that of the witness of life lived with simplicity and joy in the following of Jesus.

And third, this enormous epochal transformation shows us that we need to recover what Karl Rahner has called the "holy power of the heart." Christians are called to live friendship as a ministry. "This is my commandment, that you love one another as I have loved you" (John 15:12). In one of his books, René Voillaume tells the story of some Little Sisters of Jesus who, wishing to become friends of a group of women prisoners, asked to be allowed to share their fate. In the end, they obtained permission from the authorities to live in the prison in exactly the same conditions as the other prisoners: they kept the same rules, lived behind bars, and were supervised by guards. All the Sisters wanted was to love the prisoners to the point of sharing their fate in the most concrete way possible. They had nothing to give them except their presence and their friendship. But what changed the atmosphere in that prison completely was precisely that: the fact of those women feeling themselves touched by the Sisters being there out of friendship for them, considering their friendship something worth having. This made them believe that they were worth loving, an experience many of them had never had. So there is a revelation of Christianity that only the practice of friendship can provide. In this, the world, which can lose itself in misunderstandings about Christians, makes no mistake. Even if we are given no more than a brief moment of contact, it is enough to allow a friendship to shine through when it exists.

10

SPIRITUAL FRIENDSHIP

Our culture emphasizes love to such an extent that we very often feel unable to think properly about the forms and the place of friendship. We speak of it in monosyllables, evasively and flatly, as if we were not, after all, the inheritors of a centuries-old patrimony of experience, teaching, and words. As Marcel Proust has said, we are becoming "like that nobleman who, having shared from childhood the life of street robbers, no longer remembered his own name." We learn to see with huge telescopes the edges of the world, but we often lose the capacity to look at and understand what is closest to us. But if there is an explanation of how Christianity embedded itself in time, it is precisely friendship, and understanding it not merely as part of human formation but as a most privileged sign of the spiritual journey.

WHAT TO UNDERSTAND BY "SPIRITUAL FRIENDSHIP"

Evagrius Ponticus was the first to use the expression "spiritual friendship" in the fourth century. Having learned of a widespread philosophical culture common among monks in his day, Evagrius maintained that the Greek ideal of friendship found its fulfillment in Christian practice. But what did he understand by "spiritual friendship"? "Spiritual friendship is knowledge of God in which the saints receive the title of friends of God," he wrote in his commentary on the Book of Proverbs (n. 69). This was the title given to Moses who had spoken face-to-face with God (Exod 33:11). Again, this title was applied to John the Baptist when he was described as "the friend of the bridegroom" (John 3:29) and to the apostles themselves (John 15:15). This will be the title of all those who follow the knowledge of Christ.

Evagrius's originality consists in his not having taken human friendship as the model for divine friendship, but the opposite: the friendship that we can live with God in Jesus Christ is the model according to which we construct our human friendships. "Friendship," Evagrius goes on, "is the virtue and the knowledge of God, thanks to which we become friends of God and of the holy powers, because in this friendship the friends of one are also the friends of the other" (n. 120).

THE THIRST FOR FRIENDSHIP IS A THIRST FOR TRUTH

Later on, Saint Augustine was to exercise a decisive influence in the definition of what a "spiritual friendship" consists of, even though he did not in fact write a treatise on this topic. In his *Confessions*, his spiritual autobiography, he speaks mainly of experiences and searches. But with the existential intensity so characteristic of him, he bears witness to the way in which the thirst for friendship turns into a thirst for truth. For this reason, says Augustine, it is necessary to give oneself over to a progressive purification. Recalling his own personal experience, he confesses, "Still I did not keep the moderate way of the love of mind to mind—the bright path of friendship. Instead, the mists of passion steamed up out of the muddy concupiscence of the flesh and the hot imagination of puberty, and they so obscured and overcast my heart that I was unable to distinguish pure affection from unholy desire"

(II, 2, 2). Augustine then begins to conjugate changes in the order of grace: from comradeship to human friendship; from carnal to spiritual friendship; from the community of friends to fraternity.

To love and be loved are faculties that are both divine and human, but the only true love is that of God, because everything has its origin in him. God himself is the reason why we must love God and love one another. Our feelings often stand in the way of our living in friendship because we love as a function of the things that happen to please us. What Augustine of Hippo discovered is expressed in his own words: "There is no true friendship save between those thou dost bind together and who cleave to thee by that love which is shed abroad in our hearts through the Holy Spirit who is given to us" (IV, 4, 7). Until we have acquired this truth, we are still in that state that the author calls "fable": "to discourse and jest with him; to indulge in courteous exchanges; to read pleasant books together; to trifle together; to be earnest together; to differ at times without ill-humor,...sometimes teaching, sometimes being taught; longing for someone absent with impatience" (IV, 8, 13). However, friendship needs to be something more than a drawing room accomplishment and a smooth exercise of good manners. It is by uniting ourselves with God that we overcome the ties and equivocations that, interiorly, make us unable to go further in our search for truth. By getting close to the inner friend who is God himself, we receive from him the love that enables us to love our friends in the right way. Friendship with God thus becomes the (measureless) measure of our friendship. "Blessed is he who loves thee, and who loves his friend in thee and his enemy on account of thee" (IV, 9, 4).

It is essential for us to understand that there is nothing ethereal about this way: it is a war, a wound, an open sore in our own flesh. Augustine, for example, describes what the agonizing struggle over the loss of a friend cost him:

My heart was utterly darkened by this sorrow and everywhere I looked I saw death. My native place was a torture room to me and my father's house a strange unhappiness. And all the things I had done with him—now that he was gone—became a frightful torment....Someone spoke rightly of his friend as being "his soul's other half"—for I felt that my soul and his soul were but one soul in two bodies. Consequently, my life was now a horror to me....Not in pleasant groves, nor in sport or song, nor in fragrant bowers, nor in magnificent banquetings...not even in books or poetry did it find rest. (IV, 4, 9; 6, 11; 7, 12)

The journey to friendship in St. Augustine was to culminate in a profession of faith: "He alone loses none dear to him, if all are dear in Him who cannot be lost" (IV, 9, 14). For "Thou art Truth" (IV, 9, 14).

FRIENDSHIP IS A THEOPHANY

Twelfth-century Cistercian circles provided a further contribution of major importance for reflecting on the theology of friendship. In 1143, at the age of thirty-three, Aelred of Rievaulx was commissioned by St. Bernard to write what was to be the first of two treatises on love. *Speculum caritatis* is an apologia of evangelical monastic radicalism containing, almost like a flash of lightning, an idealization of friendship as the highest form of love. Two long decades were to pass before Aelred made more concrete this first brief reference when he dealt exclusively with spiritual friendship in his book entitled *De spirituali amicitia*. Friendship is there understood as a basic affective experience that is indispensable for our progress in the knowledge of God. To know whether God is or is not knowable, and in what way, constituted a central problem for the Cistercians. Bernard of Clairvaux, for example, contrasted knowledge of a rational order with a different form of knowledge that was not immediate but close to a mystical experience. It is at this point that Aelred puts forward a novel idea, identifying progress in the knowledge of God with the relationship of friendship. Friendship is not simply an instrument or a form of mediation between human beings and God. Friendship is rather precisely the place of encounter between the human and the divine, the place where friends can share in God, can plunge into his mystery. In this way, friendship comes to be perceived as a place of revelation. Friendship places us in God. "It is enough for one human being to become the friend of another in order to become at once a friend of God" (II, 14).

A THEOLOGY TATTOOED IN EXPERIENCE

But a theology of friendship is not merely yet another theology. Aelred states this clearly by choosing the form of dialogue for his treatise. It is as if he thereby acknowledges the impossibility of organizing a theology of friendship univocally: it is rather an intersecting polyphony, a group of various people contributing experiences, questions, forms of behavior. Not only is the existential tension not juggled with, rather it serves as a springboard for a nonabstract theological reflection, which bubbles up from the concrete and is required to pay friendly attention to it. Now, very often the concrete is a synonym of what has been tattooed in personal experience and suffering.

The relationship of friendship that Aelred's text establishes with three earlier works from classical and patristic literature is well known. Cicero's *De Amicitia* constitutes a privileged interlocutor made visible thanks to the many references Aelred makes to it, although he insists on providing a Christian interpretation of it. The other two works are the

Confessions of St. Augustine and the *De officiis* of St. Ambrose. Thinking about friendship is articulated, seeks parallels, reopens routes. But justice must be done to Aelred: although the terminology he uses does not move away from what was traditional, the meaning that he attributed to it confers on it an undeniable aura of originality. In fact, a theology of friendship is the very opposite of a closed theology.

THE SPIRITUAL TASK OF A FRIEND

Aelred argues in favor of an authentic exaltation of the spiritual role of the friend, who is described as the *custos animi*, "keeper of the soul," and *animi consors*, "soul mate, twin soul." Friendship is a school of spiritual growth. "Where such friendship exists," Aelred wrote, "there indeed is a community of likes and dislikes, the more agreeable as it is more sacred" (I, 48). The great good of spiritual friendship is precisely this: to find the trust of a heart to which you can confess your failings and reveal your progress. The spiritual friend is an image of Christ. To rest in the friend's embrace is to entrust oneself to the Holy Spirit, the life circulating in God. A friend becomes for us a master of inner detachment and freedom: "By these and similar indications emanating from the hearts of those who love and are loved in turn, through the countenance, the tongue, the eyes, and a thousand pleasing movements, to fuse our spirits by tinder, as it were, and out of many to make but one. This is what we think we should love in our friends, so that our conscience will be its own accuser if we have not loved him who in turn loves us, or if we have not returned love to him who first loved us" (III, 86). Friendship is a voluntary forgetting of oneself: "Each considers it sweet to forget himself for the sake of the other, to prefer the will of the other to one's own" (III, 132). Friendship is the authentic wisdom that always mirrors the mystery of the cross. Friendship needs both solitude and intimacy, and it is a silent agreement between souls. An authentic friendship is a form of devotion: "Thus a friend praying to Christ on behalf of his friend, and for the friend's sake desiring to be heard by Christ, directs his attention with love and longing to Christ. Without our realizing it, as it were unexpectedly, the feeling of affection passes from the friend to Christ" (III, 133). Finally, Aelred expressed the ontological value of friendship: all living beings, and not only human beings, are naturally inclined (that is to say, by divine will) to friendship, not only those who are good but also those who lack virtue. And, as Aelred himself writes, "Friendship is the perfect gift of nature and grace alike" (III, 91).

TO LOVE ON EARTH AS THEY LOVE IN HEAVEN

Some centuries later, we find many of the aspects of friendship discussed by Aelred of Rievaulx in the reflections of another great cultivator of spiritual friendship, St. Francis de Sales. In his *Introduction to the Devout Life*, he begins by locating friendship at a particular level: "Love every one with the pure love of charity, but have no friendship save with those whose intercourse is good and true" (chap. XIX). This restriction of the field defines the specificity of the relationship that friends are called upon to share. It is a question of a "partiality," but of a "holy partiality" that Francis de Sales praises as follows: "Truly it is a blessed thing to love on earth as we hope to love in Heaven, and to begin that friendship here which is to endure for ever there. I am not now speaking of simple charity, a love due to all mankind, but of that spiritual friendship which binds two or three or more souls together, leading them to share devotions and spiritual interests, so as to have but one mind between them" (XIX).

However, there is a difference in the kind of audience to which Francis de Sales and Aelred are addressing themselves. Whereas Aelred was thinking of friendship principally based on monastic practice, the former bishop of Geneva was addressing laypeople living in the world. He thought that a well-founded spiritual friendship could constitute an invaluable anchor for those wishing to grow interiorly even in the midst of the world and of the difficulties that this entails. Thus, he wrote as follows: "In the world those who aim at a devout life require to be united one with another by a holy friendship, which excites, stimulates and encourages them in well-doing" (XIX). A spiritual friendship is not a relationship designed solely to talk about Christ and the things of faith. Spiritual friendship is conducted in a conformity of the heart to Christ, but also realistically embracing life and its demands, with its diversity of times and activity. Spiritual friendship makes us more present to the present moment and to actual situations and, in the same way, does not enclose us in a small circle. It is important to remember what a near-contemporary theologian, Karl Barth, has said: "O Thou whom I encounter in my friend as an *alter ego* art in some way the gate to the whole of humanity."

SPIRITUAL BUT NOT NAÏVE

Spiritual friendship is an experience of authenticity both necessary and continuously sought. In other words, friendship needs proof, verification, and clear evangelical criteria. Unfortunately, we know of many stories of spiritual friendship that are no more than a caricature of the real thing. I remember hearing someone joking about certain situations that begin by being such an enraptured and exclusive communion of souls that they finish up in a confused and trivialized overlaying of bodies. There is no lack of examples of the transformation of these supposed spiritual friendships into unacceptable ways of dominating the other by the unacceptable use of relationships of power. However, masters of spiritual friendship such as Aelred or Francis de Sales can in no way be accused of being naïve: the one was the abbot of his monastery and the other was a bishop and an experienced spiritual director. Both knew how to identify the distortions that can influence the affective life and its manifestations. Love of God is the basis of all friendship. As Aelred wrote: "One ought to observe carefully that whatever is built thereon conforms to the foundation" (III, 5).

Great prudence is undoubtedly advisable. However, the risks inherent in friendship cannot be taken as an argument for generally regarding it with suspicion and of battling with it as if it were an evil. When built on Christ, spiritual friendship can find its solidity and timbre. Wounds and conflicts do not annihilate it, as it learns from Christ the marvelous art of hope and of forgiveness. Distance and silence do not become obstacles, since communion with Christ is alive all the time. By practicing this friendship, each one will feel the call to open him- or herself to fraternal communion in an ever wider universality that also leads us to compassion for our enemies.

11

FRIENDS, FRIENDS, BUSINESS APART?

There is no treatise on friendship that does not recommend complete detachment from material ambition. It is important not to mingle the waters. It is in this direction that Jesus' ironic comment in the parable of the unjust steward points: "Make friends for yourselves by means of dishonest wealth so that when it is gone, they may welcome you into the eternal homes" (Luke 16:9). In friendship, interest in any form of profiteering obscures what is truly good. It must be a radical experience of gratuity. We love our friend not for what he or she possesses or can give us, but simply because of what he or she is. Lanza del Vasto describes how, in one of his first pilgrimages to India, he felt that everyone approached him out of self-interest; they coveted his wallet, his watch, his camera, or his shirt. He felt he was a prisoner in that predatory relationship. In order to escape from the pressure, he went up to an isolated area where he found a lake. Delighted with the sudden release, he undressed and plunged into the calm waters of the lake. When he emerged, he realized that he had been robbed of everything, including his clothes. But he relates that, when they saw him naked, at last they accepted him as one of themselves, as a friend. It is as difficult as it is essential to achieve this level of detachment, even in our relationship with God. There is that story of a man who went into a market, leaving his bicycle at the entrance. After some time, he remembered, anxiously, that he had not collected his bicycle. What would he do without his bicycle! He raised his eyes to heaven and prayed: "Lord, if I find my bicycle, I will hurry at once to the temple to thank you." And in fact, when he emerged from the market, he found his bicycle. He at once set off for the temple where he prayed and gave thanks with tears. But when he emerged from the temple, he found his bicycle had been stolen. Friendship is the art of detachment.

FLOUR IS ONE THING, FRIENDSHIP IS ANOTHER

Some very sad stories are told about friendship. One such story is "The Devoted Friend" by Oscar Wilde. It is the story of a friendship between a fine little fellow called Hans and the rich Miller. Hans lived alone in a poor little country cottage, and every day he worked in his garden. There was no garden as lovely as his in the whole region. Flower succeeded flower so that there were always lovely things to see and lovely scents to smell.

> Little Hans had a great many friends, but the most devoted of his friends was big Hugh the Miller. Indeed, so devoted was the rich Miller to little Hans, that he would never go by his garden without leaning over the wall and plucking a large nosegay, or a handful of sweet herbs, or filling his pockets with plums and cherries if it was the fruit season.
>
> "Real friends should have everything in common," the Miller used to say, and little Hans nodded and smiled, and felt very proud of having a friend with such noble ideas.
>
> Sometimes, indeed, the neighbours thought it strange that the rich Miller never gave little Hans

anything in return, though he had a hundred sacks of flour stored away in his mill, and six milch cows, and a large flock of woolly sheep; but Hans never troubled his head about these things, and nothing gave him greater pleasure than to listen to all the wonderful things the Miller used to say about the unselfishness of true friendship.

So little Hans worked away in his garden. During the spring, the summer, and the autumn he was very happy, but when the winter came, and he had no fruit or flowers to bring to the market, he suffered a good deal from cold and hunger, and often had to go to bed without any supper but a few dried pears or some hard nuts. In the winter, also, he was extremely lonely, as the Miller never came to see him then.

"There is no good in my going to see little Hans as long as the snow lasts," the Miller used to say to his wife, "for when people are in trouble they should be left alone, and not be bothered by visitors. That at least is my idea about friendship, and I am sure I am right. So I shall wait till the spring comes, and then I shall pay him a visit, and he will be able to give me a large basket of primroses and that will make him so happy."

"You are certainly very thoughtful about others," answered the Wife, as she sat in her comfortable armchair by the big pinewood fire.

"But could we not ask little Hans up here?" said the Miller's youngest son. "If poor Hans is in trouble I will give him half my porridge, and show him my white rabbits."

"What a silly boy you are!" cried the Miller. "I really don't know what is the point of sending you to school. You seem not to learn anything. Why, if little Hans came up here, and saw our warm fire, and our good supper, and our great cask of red wine, he might get envious, and envy is a most terrible thing, and would spoil anybody's nature. I certainly will not allow Hans' nature to be spoiled. I am his best friend, and I will always watch over him, and see that he is not led into any temptations. Besides, if Hans came here, he might ask me to let him have some flour on credit, and that I could not do. Flour is one thing, and friendship is another, and they should not be confused."

A story such as this could only have a sad ending, which I will not relate, leaving my readers to seek it out for themselves. But let us not forget: the most powerful image of life is a ring of friendship, and it is in this that we all stand, holding hands with one another. Inclusion represents not only a value, but a necessary condition. Hands almost seem to burst into flower when they are opened. Arms in a sense grow longer when they are opened for an embrace. Bread multiplies itself when it allows itself to be shared. The true grammar of life is sharing.

IS IT ONLY ON THE BAKER'S SELF-INTEREST THAT WE CAN COUNT?

The father of modern economics, Adam Smith, summarized the way the economic system works in the following pragmatic statement: "It is not from the benevolence of the baker that we expect our dinner, but from his regard for his own interest." It is thanks to the hope of gain that the goods that we need appear on the supermarket shelves. Moreover, the truth of this statement is commonly accepted. However, the fact that is given prominence today with increasing urgency is quite different. Obviously, the legitimate expectation that one's work should prove profitable remains perfectly valid, but the problem that our societies are being called upon to resolve, albeit far from completely, is the question of the inequalities that these societies generate and that threaten to destroy them. Now, this process of readjustment and perfecting of the system clearly cannot depend exclusively on what Adam Smith called "the baker's greed." The difficult situation we now face shows us, without a shadow of doubt, how important and indeed vital it has become to introduce basic alternatives in a field that is both economic and financial, but is also human and civilizational.

WHAT HAS YOUR MONEY DONE TO YOU?

Our Western world has erected such an impenetrable barrier between the spiritual and the material that, from the very beginning, it has made obtuse any dialogue between spirituality and the production and circulation of wealth, let alone any discussion of the functioning of the economy or the various kinds of capitalism. They are completely separate fields of activity. Or, at best, money has now come to occupy the place of the sacred. This being so, the prophetic challenge issued by the philosopher Jacques Ellul is extremely pertinent: "We must make money profane," that is, restore it to its function as a material instrument of exchange, stripping it of the symbolic sacredness with which it is treated.

Here, too, the reading of the Bible can be instructive. The Old Testament, for example, has a fundamentally positive appreciation of goods and of prosperity. But the difference between the rich and the poor is always seen as an intolerable scandal. All the social legislation contained in the Book of Deuteronomy is not in terms of recommending the giving of alms but rather (and courageously) of defending the rights of the poor. In the so-called Law of the Covenant, it establishes a genuine social contract that decrees astonishingly concrete measures such as the remission of debts in a periodic redistribution of goods as a means of breaking the cyclic phenomena of the impoverishment of the weakest social groups.

At times, we hear the phrase "Render to Caesar the things that are Caesar's and to God the things that are God's" (see Matt 22:21) as indicating that Jesus turned his back on money. The Gospel does not tell us this. The episode in the house of Zacchaeus, the rich tax collector, shows, on the contrary, how what happens is a change of roles. The money ceases to be heaped up and used for him alone, and becomes instead the means of making good injustice and an antidote to poverty. As the theologian Daniel Marguerat has explained, Jesus' intervention takes us much further, because he does not merely ask, "What are you doing with your money," but confronts us with an unavoidable question: "What has your money done to you?"

In his encyclical *Caritas in Veritate*, Pope Benedict XVI challenges us to apply to the economy, too, the logic of gratuitousness and gift: "Gratuitousness is present in our lives in many different forms, which often go unrecognized because of a purely consumerist and utilitarian view of life. The human being is made for gift, which expresses and makes present his transcendent dimension....Economic, social and political development, if it is to be authentically human, needs to make room for the *principle of gratuitousness* as an expression of fraternity" (n. 34).

12

IN PRAISE OF
GRATUITOUSNESS

I once read, and I have never forgotten, something that Clarice Lispector wrote about one of those sudden happenings that can save a life: she calls it, quite rightly, a "gratuitous act." Maybe we need to begin by explaining what such an act is not. It is not yet another stopping place on the breathless battle for life that keeps us on the move from day to day. It is not the necessary rush to work, to possessions, to meals, to the implacable timetable for appointments, to catch buses or trains that go on forever. Nor can it be identified with those small pleasures that we allow ourselves, the short breaks, the organized trips, the rewards for this or that. A "gratuitous act" is priceless: by definition, it can neither be bought nor paid for.

It is always a thirst for freedom that alerts us to the gratuitous. And it is not freedom from this or that. I would say it is, above all, a pure freedom to be, to feel alive; an expansion of the soul, unconditioned by the greediness of conventions; an urgent need not for gifts, but to give. Today, for example, a friend came to ask me to recommend a form of voluntary work for her. She does not have much time, as she has a demanding and complex job and has children at the age at which they are very dependent on her. "Perhaps I can only offer two hours every two weeks," she said to me. I replied, smiling: "Two hours can be an immense amount of time." In fact, time is not the most important thing. The essential thing is to release what is at work within us and to express freely the "gratuitous act."

Acts of service to others are an excellent example of the gratuitous. However, they must also exist in relation to us. In the piece by Clarice Lispector that I read, she wrote,

> It was two o'clock on a summer's afternoon. I interrupted my work, quickly changed, went downstairs, hailed a taxi and said to the driver: "Drop me off at the Botanical Gardens." "Where is that?" he asked. "You don't understand," I explained. "It's not a street or a district. I mean the Gardens in the 'bairro'." I don't know why, but he looked at me very closely for a moment.
>
> I opened the windows of the car, which was going very fast, and I had already begun my freedom, allowing a strong wind to toss my hair and blow into my face grateful for freedom. What was I on my way to the Botanical Gardens for? Just to look. Just to see. Just to feel. Just to live.

DO YOU BELIEVE IN LIFE BEFORE DEATH?

I once saw scrawled on a wall the following question: "Do you believe in life before death?" It shook me. Clearly, to believe in life after death widens our horizon considerably. However, if I, for some reason, cease to believe that there is such a thing as life (that is, the possibility of a true life) before my death, everything becomes strange, dark, and lost.

The "gratuitous act" is a gesture that saves us. We know this so well in the living out of a friendship! The gratuitous releases us from the dictatorship of aims that end up by preventing us from living authentically. Gratuitousness is to live immersed in being. It gives us access to the polyphony of life in all its variety, in its contrasts, in the denseness of its reality, in its entirety.

Jesus is the master of the gratuitous. When we read the Gospels in this key, we find it appearing in the words of Jesus. He led each one back to make of the obstacle a fundamental opening for an encounter and, at bottom, for a fundamental opening to a life in accordance with one's own being. Very often, our prayer still emerges as if it were a useful space, and not as a place of gratuitous and essential friendship, where soul and body can breathe.

ROOM FOR AUTHENTICITY

I am delighted, truly delighted, that the first words spoken by Jesus in St. John's Gospel are a question (and that particular question): "What are you looking for?" (John 1:38). It comforts me to realize that what upholds the architecture of the meetings and missed meetings related in the Gospels is a kind of choreography of questions, an intense exchange of questions constructed tentatively in most cases, with no clear idea, full of doubts, with many misfired shots, much difficulty in even communicating. This is an anchor, albeit a costly one, as a life resting solely on answers is a diminished life, like a springtime that never actually blooms. I do not know how springtime will make its appearance in us, how this reflowering that nature insinuates will come about, this rebirth that Jesus' paschal gesture amazingly brings (back) to life in our humanity. All I do know is that by asking questions, even those that are difficult and that cost us dearly, we rediscover life made manifest and open, undoubtedly more fragile, but the only life that enables us to touch the edges of an authentic existence.

All of us are full of questions and they draw maps of areas of silence, the frontier areas of our being. Just recently, I once again read Pilate's question (also in St. John's Gospel): "What is truth?" (18:38). And I took it into my head to compare this question with one of Jesus' characteristic phrases: "I am the way, and the truth, and the life" (John 14:6). Without wishing to relativize the densely dogmatic nature of this saying, I nevertheless decided to have another look at it from the existential angle. It was as if Jesus, a master of life who is constantly reformulating himself in us, were challenging us to an appropriation. Yes, to an appropriation. Faced with so many ways already followed and yet to be followed, it is necessary for each one of us to say: "I am the way I am following." It is essential that the truth that we accept should not be a super-imposition but a deep expression of what we are: "I am the truth." It is urgent that life should not be merely an accumulation of time and its sleep-ridden progress but that each one, at least once, can really and truly say: "I am the life." Is not this the deep impact of the friendship that Jesus has with us?

13

LOVING IMPERFECTION

I have often heard the poet Tonino Guerra quote the words of a medieval monk: "We must move beyond mere perfection." In friendship, it is precisely this that confronts us: perfection can be a path that we tread superficially, or an illusion that prevents us from gaining access to what is real and true. We spend so much time even in losing the mania of perfect things, perfect persons, and curing ourselves of the impulse that exiles us in the seeming comfort of idealizations, or ultimately in overcoming the vice of superimposing on reality a cortège of comfortable (but false) images. "We must move beyond mere perfection."

Perfection confronts us with reality as if it were a question of dealing with something that has actually happened: if we were to mix, to intervene, to touch up or alter, we experience this as a disturbance. This perfection is static. It exists merely to be admired—at a distance. Friendship built on this basis is consumed by a narcissistic tension: we choose "friends" on account of their importance, their status, their appearance. We make of friendship a desire for applause. I recall that passage in Saint-Exupéry's *Little Prince* in which he visits a planet occupied by a conceited man:

> "Do you really admire me very much?" He demanded of the little prince.
> "What does that mean—'admire'?"
> "To admire means that you regard me as the

handsomest, the best-dressed, the richest, and the most intelligent man on this planet."

"But you are the only man on your planet!"

"Do me this kindness. Admire me just the same."

"I admire you," said the little prince, shrugging his shoulders slightly, "but what is there in that to interest you so much?"

To welcome imperfection is to accept friendship as an unfinished history, one that includes ourselves actively in the telling. In imperfection, it is always possible to begin and begin again. Imperfection enables us to understand singularity, diversity, the real impact of the passage of time in each one. It is true that our own frailties sometimes enable us to see our singularities. It is the impact of frailty in us that reveals our deepest reality, shows us the life of God and his footprints. In this sense, imperfection makes us human. To welcome it is a necessary condition in friendship, and in the personal growth to maturity that we must achieve. The most urgent thing is to learn to sow, in a work of ever-greater trust, detachment, and simplicity. I love this poem by Adília Lopes:

If you love me on account of beauty, then you don't
    love me!
Love the Sun which has golden hair!
If you love me on account of youth, then you don't
    love me!
Love the Spring which is new every year!
If you love me on account of riches, then you don't
    love me!
Love the Woman of the Sea: she has many bright
    pearls!
If you love me on account of intelligence, then you
    don't love me!
Love Isaac Newton: he wrote the
Philosophiae Naturalis Principia Mathematica!

But if you love me for the sake of love, then yes indeed,
    you do love me!
Love me always: I love you for always!

LOVE AND TRUTH HAVE MET

In the first great meeting with Jesus, Peter said to him:
"Go away from me, Lord, for I am a sinful man!" (Luke 5:8). We
are all injured, opaque, incomplete. We all of us carry within
ourselves a countless number of stifled dreams, of foolish dis-
putes, of words we never managed to say, of an inner violence,
whether diffused or concentrated. Even our happiness is
mixed in with the memory of unhappinesses that still burn
within us, even though we stifle them. We are truer to ourselves, however, when we acknowledge all this and when we
share it all in the confidence of a friendship. The mechanisms
of self-defense and culpabilisation only isolate us even further.
And, as Jesus explains to Peter, holiness is not a lack of sinful-
ness, but that movement deep within us to turn toward
another, toward the Totally Other, and allow ourselves to be
traversed by an experience of gratitude and mercy as, in the
darkness of a cathedral, the stained glass window lets the light
come through. Hence, our petition must be this: "Come close
to me, for I am a sinner," daring to use this necessary and rare
form of audacity that is humility. Psalm 84 (85) contains this
marvelous image: "Love and faithfulness meet together; righteousness and peace kiss each other" (v. 11 [10]).

OUR HUMANITY IS
GOD'S NARRATIVE

One of the most liberating human and spiritual experiences is when we gain the strength to thank God: "I praise
you, for I am fearfully and wonderfully made" (Ps 138[9]:14). In
fact, our humanity tells God's story: our face tells us how his

face is; our hands let us see his; he speaks in our words, and the more open our gestures are, the better he breathes; our eyes reveal how his eyes sparkle; our silences and our laughter are maps for those who wish to reach him. Our frailty reveals the power of his compassion. The absences in which we lose ourselves make it possible to perceive ever more clearly his friendship. Like any mother or father, he does not want his son or daughter to be taller or shorter, fair or dark. All he wants is for his children to be what they are to the full. There is nothing in us that is either unknown or indifferent to him: interruptions and new beginnings, frustrations and challenges, times of turbulence or tranquility. He arrives at all hours, without ever going away. He enters when we open the door to him, but he is always there present. He is here and he is there. He is embracing us now and at the same time, he is waiting to enfold us in the embrace without end.

14

THE LITTLE GOSPEL OF JOY

Let us go back to thinking about joy. Halfway through this journey that is our life, let us reflect on our joy, let us seek its secret roots. At the beginning of St. Luke's Gospel, there is a refrain that is proclaimed extremely clearly by angels from heaven. This refrain constitutes a kind of mini-Gospel, transparent and unrestricted, like the one who comes down from heaven; and it is also, in a way, a summary of the Gospel as a whole. It is proclaimed by the angels who say to the shepherds: "I am bringing you good news of great joy for all people!" (Luke 2:10). In essence, every Christian proclamation is this: the experience of a joy that is addressed to everyone: "I am bringing you good news of great joy for all people!" Hence, joy places us at the very center of the Christian mystery. It is as if our faith journey would be incomplete if we did not plunge eagerly right to the bottom of this Gospel of Joy.

THE JOY THAT THRILLS US

But what is joy? Joy cannot be reduced to a form of well-being or an emotional consolation, though it may well be expressed in this way. Fundamentally, joy is a deep expression of our being: in goodness, in truth, in beauty, an expression of our being to the full. St. Luke's way of describing joy in Jesus is interesting. His joy is described as "being deeply stirred." It seems a magnificent and precise way of expressing it, since it is precisely this: pure thrill, the expression of the whole of one's being, a manifestation of the soul. "Jesus rejoiced in the Holy Spirit and said: 'I thank thee, Father, Lord of heaven and earth, because you have hidden these things from the wise and the intelligent and have revealed them to infants'" (Luke 10:21).

We rejoice, moved by the thrill of the joy within us. And Jesus, too, rejoices in the same way, giving thanks to the Father. As the stem of a flower trembles in the breeze, as the flower itself trembles when bathed in light, so we too are called to this silent and surprising thrill of life.

WHAT HAVE WE DONE WITH THE GOSPEL OF JOY?

Joy is a very personal and profound opening out of oneself. There are no two joys alike, as there are no two tears or sorrows that are alike. Joy is a grammar in the singular. On the one hand, it has a physical expression, but on the other, it retains also a clearly spiritual nature. Joy, we might say, is an arousing of the spirit that takes us close to miracle, to this miracle that, in the mouth of Jesus, is expressed in these words: "I bless you, Father." The miracle is to recognize that the Father is the origin of the enigma that we are, and that this is expressed in praise, in song, in beatitude, in laughter, in the sharing of enthusiasm. It is to open a door, a pathway, a corridor for the passing of the spirit. In this sense, joy, which is the intimate condition of friends, is also a way of living to be assumed. We are called to live in joy.

However, in theological and ecclesiastical circles, joy has become a theme that is dealt with rather sparingly. We say very little about the Gospel of Joy, and it rarely appears amongst all that we undertake as a duty, as a task. It is not so very often that we are reminded, as we should be, of the duty of joy, of being committed every day to joy, sent forth in the name of joy. Our liturgies, sermons, catecheses, and pastoral work approach joy almost bashfully. And it may well be that the passages from the Bible that come most readily to our minds are not those that speak of joy. In other words, in our spiritual traditions and practices, joy has become a topic that is more or less marginal, a kind of subtheme and, at times, one that is as it were under a kind of interdict. Nietzsche used to say that Christianity would be more credible if Christians were seen to be cheerful. And, in fact, the public image of Christianity seems to be more focused on duty, severity, to the point of intransigence in moral matters rather than in the simplicity of the Gospel of Joy. What have we done with the Gospel of Joy?

OUR DIFFICULTY IN FINDING JOY

Let us go back to the year 1975. It was a Holy Year, and the Apostolic Exhortation for this Holy Year signed by Pope Paul VI began with these words: *Gaudete in Domino* ("Rejoice in the Lord"). They are words that come from St. Paul's letter to the Philippians: "Rejoice in the Lord always; again I will say, Rejoice" (4:4). The picture that Paul VI presents at the beginning of this exhortation is interesting. He says:

> This difficulty in finding joy seems to us particularly acute today. Technological society has succeeded in multiplying the opportunities for pleasure, but it has great difficulty in generating joy. For joy comes from another source. It is spiritual. Money, comfort, hygiene, and material security are often not lacking, and yet boredom, depression, and sadness unhappily remain the lot of many. This generates anguish and the despair which feverish consumerism, the frantic search for immediate happiness and for artificial paradises cannot assuage.

When all is said and done, our culture lives out of step with joy. We travel along routes, which proclaim on the one hand our longing for joy, but at the same time our inability to plunge into the depths of joy, true joy. However, faced with this picture of a failure to find joy, Paul VI does not refrain from concluding, "This situation nevertheless cannot hinder us from speaking about joy and hoping for joy." In fact, our diagnosis of the world around us cannot silence the Gospel of Joy.

JOY IS AN APPRENTICESHIP

We define ourselves as *homo faber*, the artisan, the manufacturer, those who fulfill themselves in what they do. And we distance ourselves from the horizon of the *homo festivus*, that is, those who are capable of celebrating, those who take creation to its fullness. We see this in the opening of the Book of Genesis. God begins the work of Creation and brings it to completion in the space of six days, and on the seventh day God rests. Now the rest is neither an appendage nor an appropriate ending to the Creation. The rest, this *Shabbat*, is the moment of joy and contemplation; it is the moment for falling in love and for enjoyment; it is the moment for rejoicing! In fact, our activity remains incomplete if it consists in pure activism, in repeated doing. Blessed are those who arrange flowers in a vase and then pause in delight. The worst thing that can happen to us is to have a life in which we are doing things, which may well be good and necessary things, but in which we have lost the capacity for delight, for contemplation and pleasure. These are the ways that enable the eyes to perceive the meaning, to feel fulfillment. Joy does not come when we stop living; joy comes to birth when we seize hold of any one of its many threads, and are capable of following it faithfully to its fullness. Its fullness is always this culminating moment.

God creates "and saw that it was good" or, according to the Septuagint, "And he saw that it was beautiful." God does not merely create. God creates and sees that his Creation is incomplete without joy, without delight, without our feeling that what we have collaborated in, what we have helped to plan, that of which we have been creators and witnesses demands of us this moment of pure gratuitousness in which we perceive the fragment in the whole; we perceive the particle in the totality; we inscribe time in eternity. We neither separate, nor divide. We realize that a word is as important as a book. An hour in the garden can be as important as an hour of adoration. Why? Because we have the capacity to aim for, and allow ourselves to be pointed toward, this crowning moment.

Kierkegaard used to say, "Anguish is our deadly disease." Anguish is the poison that corrodes us. Anguish is that fear that paralyzes us, that lack of security that depresses us, that does not let us be, that does not allow our soul to expand in its peace, its originality. Anguish is a mortal disease. Joy is the health of the soul. Hence the proverb that says, "A sad saint is a sorry saint." Joy is a vital thermometer. And if we are continually irritated, sad, full of complaints, talking more about the things that weigh us down than about the things that delight us, then there is an inner re-awakening that must be brought about. For joy, too, can be learned.

PAIN DIGS IN US A VOID THAT WILL LATER BE FILLED WITH JOY

When speaking of joy, we all know that it is a kind of unfinished symphony. There is that poem by Khalil Gibran, in *The Prophet*, in which joy and sorrow look at each other:

> When you are joyous, look deep into your heart and you shall find it is only that which has given you sorrow that is giving you joy. When you are sorrowful look again in your heart, and you shall see that in truth you are weeping for that which has been your delight. Some of you say: "Joy is greater than sorrow,"

and others say, "Nay, sorrow is the greater." But I say unto you, they are inseparable, they come together.

That is how we feel joy; we feel it like scales, the rise and fall of which we cannot avoid. In this sense, joy is this fragile gift, this gift that often has a kind of affinity with suffering and pain. As the poem teaches us, it is not wise to create oppositions because the lute was made with a pocketknife, after which it produces an incredible music. Very often, it is the pain that digs out depths in us that will later be filled with joy. In this sense, joy is the daughter and the fruit of hope.

IT IS EASIER TO BE PESSIMISTIC

Western tradition leaves no room for doubt in the link it has established between wisdom and pessimism. One of those unforgettable portraits of Rembrandt suffices to tell us everything: the wise person is the one seated in the shadows, looking from afar at the illusions of transparency. This is something that has not changed. Just think about how much more easily the serious person is deemed to be wise rather than a joyful one. A tortured and reticent spirit receives more appreciation and applause than all those who do their best to keep hope alive.

In fact, there is an error of assessment that tends to regard the cheerful person's joy as a spontaneous expression of his or her character, one that owes nothing to the person's spiritual journey and growth to maturity. In fact, we experience the precise opposite of this, since in many cases pessimism is the easiest response to the pressure of time. Clearly, pessimism exercises a purifying function in relation to our sidetracking, but in a world governed by pessimists, we would not even be encouraged to raise anchor in the harbor. Joy does not hide from us the reasons for pessimism, but enables us to integrate the entire human reality in a wider and patient project in which obstacles may actually be opportunities.

FRIENDSHIP IS A SOURCE OF JOY

"Who is the third who walks always beside you?" Whenever I come across this question, taken from "The Wasteland" by T. S. Eliot, I almost always think of friends. A friend, by definition, is someone who walks beside us, even when we are separated by thousands of miles or several score years. Separation and distance are completely relativized by the practice of friendship. The same is true of silence and the word. A friend brings together these conditions that seem paradoxical: he or she is at the same time the person to whom we can tell everything and the one in whose company we can remain in silence for long periods without any embarrassment. We certainly have friends of both types. With some, our friendship is sealed in the capacity to pour out the story of our lives, to describe little happenings, to identify in words the light that enlightens us. With others, the friendship is fundamentally a great capacity to listen, as if what we say were always no more than the visible tip of a marvelous hidden inner world that cannot be expressed in words.

What feeds a friendship also provides food for thought. It is striking to note how it evokes in us such delightful and deep signs with disconcerting simplicity: an exchange of glances (but which we experience as an exchange of greetings in our soul), a quality of listening, a very brief—or month-long—period of sharing, or a conversation, a mutual commitment in a project, an artless and profound joy. A friend is someone capable of perceiving, if only for a moment, the smile, whether open or hidden, that each one of us carries in the depths of our heart. A friend is a shepherd and a master of our smile. The poet Patrice De La Tour du Pin has written:

Begin by conquering joy,
go two by two
to protect yourselves from evil,
through the forests,

beside the rivers,
along all the roads that are open in the solitude of light
you must seek for joy.

How do friends seek joy? And what testimony do they convey to our heart?

1. The knowledge that we are committed to joy

A friend is the one who often reminds us that we are committed to joy. In St. John's Gospel, Jesus said, "I have said these things to you so that my joy may be in you, and that your joy may be complete" (15:11). He also said, "No one will take your joy from you" (John 16:22). There is a joy that no one and nothing can take from us, and that constitutes the horizon of our lives.

When we look at what we are and where we live, when we look toward the end of the journey that we are making, it is important that we feel called to joy. It is toward the circle of the Blessed that we are walking. For this reason, we are tirelessly moving our heart from the weight of the shadow to the clarity of the light. In fact, we are shot through, we are being guided, led by the hand of a promise, and this promise is joy. We do not know what this is. For now, our joy is only partial, provisional, it is as yet the joy of this moment, this instant; however, the joy that is promised to us is a complete joy.

Friendship is this exchange of glances that says to life that it is committed to joy. "But I feel so weighed down"; "I am in so much pain"; "But I feel I am condemned; I condemn myself; I feel there is no salvation for me, no means of rescue"; "I am in a blind alley and there is no way out." Whatever our current situation, let us feel ourselves committed to joy. Joy is the promise. As Dietrich Bonhoeffer once said: "God does not grant all our wishes, but He does fulfill his promises."

2. Joy is a form of hospitality

One of the characteristic features of joy is the fact that it does not belong to us. It is highly personal. It is completely ours, identifies itself with us, but it does not belong to us. Joy passes through us. Joy is always a gift. Joy is born of the act of welcoming. Joy is born when I am willing to build my life in an atmosphere of hospitality. If I make my living space sound-proof, if I seal off my readiness to pay attention, joy will not come visiting. Joy is a gift of friendship welcomed.

Joy is not programmed. For example, I cannot say that I am going to laugh in a minute, nor do I know when the next time that I shall laugh will be. Joy is a gift that pays me surprise visits, never ones that have been planned. In this sense, I have to live in a spirit of welcome. My heart is a threshold, a half-open door. My life lives on the welcoming of friends. We have become porous, let ourselves be touched, let ourselves be carried on the refreshing flow of life. There is an Ingmar Bergman film in which one of the characters is a young girl who is anorexic—and we all know that anorexia is a form of detachment from one's own life, of distancing oneself from all affectivity. The girl goes to see a doctor, and this is what he tells her, and it is something that applies to each one of us: "Look here, there is only one remedy for you, only one way forward: every day allow yourself to be touched by someone or by something." Joy is this readiness to be welcoming.

Days in which there is no joy are simply not remembered. We get to the end of the day and we do not remember a single gesture, a single moment, a single encounter, a single act or action, we have nothing to relate. I have had to see to and to listen to many things, and to be with many people, but I did not want either the one or the other; I did not let there be any channel or means of communication, I did not open my heart. We need to transform our lives in the direction of hospitality. Friendship teaches us this.

114

3. Only a simple heart is capable of joy

There is no joy without innocence. But innocence in the sense indicated by the writer Cristina Campo: "We are not born innocent, but we can die innocent." The innocence of spiritual childhood is that innocence with which and through which we can die: the innocence of a simple heart, of gratuitousness, of trust.

If I have not the heart of a child, I am not an heir of the kingdom of God. That is to say, I am not an heir of the kingdom of life. I do not see the sparkle, I do not catch a glimpse. In this, children are our models because they amuse themselves with little nothings, which at bottom are the serious things, the things from which they catch the light. This is what we need. We need this childhood, to discover childhoods within ourselves. It is not by chance that all friends are friends of childhood, even those whom we meet later in life. The principal childhood to bear witness to is this future one.

Instead of growing in severity, in intransigence, in indifference, in sarcasm, in backbiting, in complaining, let us walk quietly in the opposite direction. Let us grow in simplicity, in gratitude, in detachment, and in confidence. Joy has to do with the essentials that can only be welcomed in spiritual poverty.

15

GOD'S SENSE OF HUMOR

If we say that God is Love, no one is astonished. Indeed, repetition has made the statement banal. But if we hear someone say that God is Humor, we are on the alert because we feel that someone is trying to get into God's domain "by the back door" and not through the front door. The truth is that friendship does not dispense with humor.

Our ability to bear witness is often held hostage to a foolish *gravitas*, to a seriousness that easily turns into a weight. And yet, the Bible is a kind of grammar of God's humor. Incredible as it may seem, that extremely serious collection of books is also full of humor, although this dimension of the Bible is rarely alluded to and taught. There are pages that constitute a pure alphabet of joy and many moments that can only be understood by those who burst out laughing. The fact is that God's revelation is proclaimed in a dynamic that is clearly joyful.

Perhaps we have to take seriously the playful verse that Psalm 2:4 whispers to us: "He who sits in the heavens laughs." Or recognize that the word *believer* is called upon to open up like a festive choreography, as is described in Psalm 33: "Rejoice in the LORD . . . praise the LORD with the lyre; make melody to him with the harp of ten strings. Sing to him a new song; play skillfully on the strings, with loud shouts" (1–3).

Along the same lines is the marvelous image we find in the Book of Proverbs (8:30–31) that presents Wisdom, the emanation of God, his visible presence, to us as follows: Divine

116

Wisdom is "rejoicing before him always, rejoicing in his inhabited world and delighting in the children of men" (ESV). It is a disconcerting declaration, and we are still far from taking it in, such is the challenge that it represents. It is not in the series of tasks traditionally linked with wisdom (judging, thinking, scrutinizing, foreseeing, and so on) that we find the Wisdom of God. Its program is infinitely simpler: to play, to delight in the children of men.

So let us look at the Bible and amuse ourselves in reading it, experiencing the way in which joy is a place for revealing the friendship of God. It is impossible to come close to God without becoming aware of this indispensable dimension. In the Bible, we find pages full of a humor that is represented and transmitted in many different ways.

GOD MADE ME LAUGH

A characteristic text is the story of Abraham and his wife, Sarah. In their story of faith, laughter and humor come naturally to the fore. There is the background that we all know: Sarah was sterile and the couple was elderly and childless. Into this situation comes God's unexpected promise: that within a year, Sarah will be a mother. And Sarah, when she overhears this, laughs to herself within the tent.

> The LORD said to Abraham, "Why did Sarah laugh, and say, 'Shall I indeed bear a child, now that I am old?' Is anything too wonderful for the LORD? At the set time I will return to you, in due season, and Sarah shall have a son." But Sarah denied, saying, "I did not laugh"; for she was afraid. He said, "Oh yes, you did laugh." (Gen 18:13–15)

What the Lord says is delightful, and will determine the name of the child to be born. For the name Isaac means "God laughs." To begin with, Sarah laughed out of incredulity, in pure disbelief when faced with God's disconcerting promise, for she cannot see how it can be fulfilled. But she is challenged to laugh precisely in this context, perceiving how God's humor removes the barriers from the history of impasses and deadlocks, and makes possible what she, in her heart, felt was impossible. She is going to have a son, and can say, "God has brought laughter for me; everyone who hears will laugh with me" (Gen 21:6). A completely new laugh: that of trust in the unforeseeable ways of God.

LAUGHTER LEADS US TO WISDOM

Often we find laughter associated with the construction of true wisdom. The Bible teaches us to laugh at our judgments and knowledge, at the deeply serious things that we do, at the skill with which we endeavor to keep up appearances or overcome difficulties. This laughter at ourselves is a highly purifying laughter and opens us to a new feeling, to another smile, which is that of God. Above all, in the Wisdom books, we find a series of maxims to be read with a smile on our lips, because they decidedly strip us naked:

> Do not consult with a woman about her rival
> or with a coward about war,
> with a merchant about business
> or with a buyer about selling,
> with a miser about generosity
> or with the merciless about kindness,
> with an idler about any work…
> with a lazy servant about a big task.
>
> (Sir 37:11)

When we read this advice in the Book of Sirach, we laugh to ourselves because we recognize our own reality, but the laughter purifies us, opens us to a profound knowledge of ourselves. Laughter serves as a mirror: instead of concealing ourselves in a kind of hide-and-seek of appearances, it opens up to us the possibility of an undramatic contemplation that constructively urges us to change our ways:

> The lazy person says, "There is a lion in the road!
>   There is a lion in the streets!"
> As a door turns on its hinges,
>   so does a lazy person in bed.
> The lazy person buries a hand in the dish,
> and is too tired to bring it back to the mouth.
>   (Prov 26:13–15)

> A continual dripping on a rainy day
> and a contentious wife are alike.
>   (Prov 27:15)

> The leech has two daughters;
> "Give, give," they cry.
>   (Prov 30:15)

Sirach and Proverbs are filled with maxims that are inspired to a considerable extent by Middle Eastern–style humor, which in some ways differs considerably from our own. But the important thing is to realize that laughter is a wise way of entering into ourselves, into our real selves, to break down the false solidity of appearances, daring to see ourselves as we really are. In this sense, laughter has a sapiential function: it is a means of entering into spiritual wisdom, it leads us to it.

In the Bible, there are quite a few masters of outrageous excuses. When Moses descended from the Mount of Revelation and re-appeared with the Tablets of the Law, he had the surprise of his life! What he expected was to find the people all of one heart and one mind in readiness for receiving the Law. Instead, he found them all gathered around a golden calf! Moses demanded an explanation from Aaron, as we are told in chapter 32 of the Book of Exodus. And Aaron uttered the most outrageous excuse in the Bible. He said, "They wanted a god, they gave me gold, I threw it into the fire, and out came this calf." It is interesting because the Book of Exodus, in addition to being an account of the liberation, is also an amusing story. We do not attain our freedom without accepting the nonsense within us.

WE SHOULD "SEASON" OUR PRAYER WITH HUMOR

Laughter helps us to go beyond the fatalism that at times assails us violently. The earlier text in Genesis 18 is an excellent example. Here, Abraham tries to persuade God to save the city of Sodom, which was about to be condemned. Abraham built up a strategy. First he said: "Will you indeed sweep away the righteous with the wicked? Suppose there are fifty righteous within the city; will you then sweep away the place and not forgive it for the fifty righteous who are in it?" Abraham clearly knew that there were not fifty righteous men in Sodom, but if God were to say yes, God would have entered into the game! There are times when the problem is this: to join in the game! We see this clearly in Jesus' parables! Jesus frequently induces the people to enter into the game of his logic and, once they have done that, the surprise of the kingdom of God can break in. God's reply to Abraham is, "If I find at Sodom fifty righteous in the city, I will forgive the whole place for their sake." Abraham then suggests a ten percent discount, and says, "Suppose five of the fifty righteous are lacking? Will you destroy the whole city for lack of five?" In a text filled with humor, Abraham, encouraged, goes on pleading, for thirty, twenty, and on down to ten righteous. Here we recognize the purpose of the game, which at bottom is a question of humor.

At times, our prayer is too serious. It is very important that it should be laced with humor. To learn to pray like Sarah and Abraham, with these two believers, is to learn to pray with our laughter, with our problems and feelings of disbelief, with this kind of good-humored game that prayer brings with it. There is such a great lack of proportion between heaven and earth, between the fidelity of God and our own frailty that, when all is said and done, and through it all, only God's smile printed on our faces can make the difference. It was for a reason that the father of the prodigal son arranged for his house to ring with music and dancing (see Luke 15:25).

HUMOR AND PROPHECY

Humor is also essential in order to understand the prophets and the prophetic vocation. We have immense admiration for the prophets, but in many cases, when God called them from the place where they were, the first thing they did was to take no notice! God spoke and they did nothing—just like ourselves. God said to Amos, "Behold, I want you to go and prophesy," and Amos replied, "I am no prophet, nor a prophet's son; but I am a herdsman" (Amos 7:14). When God asked Jeremiah to be his prophet, Jeremiah replied, "I do not know how to speak, for I am only a boy" (Jer 1:6). God laughs at our objections, transforming what seemed to us insuperable obstacles! God's humor accompanies us throughout our lives.

Just look at the example recorded in the Book of Jonah, which is perhaps the great book of biblical humor. God said, "Go at once to Nineveh, that great city, and cry out against it: for their wickedness has come up before me" (1:2), and he sent Jonah southward. But Jonah immediately tried to escape—by heading north! While still fleeing, he boarded a ship that got into difficulties, and he was eventually swallowed by a whale. When he escaped from this predicament (for the whale vomited him out), there followed the episode of the plant. The prophet was sleeping comfortably under a bush and suddenly it withered. When the sun beat down on him, he once again rebelled against God.

Thus, we see how the prophets convey God's revelation by the amusing tenor of their own lives. If each of us were to write his or her own life story, the love and humor of God would be clearly linked.

CONVERSION BY HUMOR

Chapter 18 of the first Book of Kings is a wonderful text. It relates the story of the prophet Elijah, who met with God not in thunder or lightning, or in wind or earthquake, but in a still small voice, a gentle breeze. This Elijah was the only one to stand up against an army of four hundred priests of Baal, in a competition to see which of them would be defended by their god. Starting from an archaic religiosity that is very close to polytheism, we see how important God's sense of humor was in building the paradigm of the true believer:

> Then Elijah said to the people, "I, even I only, am left a prophet of the LORD; but Baal's prophets number four hundred and fifty. Let two bulls be given to us; let them choose one bull for themselves, cut it in pieces, and lay it on the wood, but put no fire to it; I will prepare the other bull and lay it on the wood, but put no fire to it. Then you call on the name of your god and I will call on the name of the LORD; the god who answers by fire is indeed God." All the people answered, "Well spoken!" Then Elijah said to the prophets of Baal, "Choose for yourselves one bull and prepare it first, for you are many; then call on the name of your god, but put no fire to it." So they took the bull that was given them, prepared it, and called on the name of Baal from morning until noon, crying, "O Baal, answer us!" But there was no voice, and no answer. They limped about the altar that they had made. At noon Elijah mocked them, saying, "Cry aloud! Surely he is a god; either he is

meditating, or he has wandered away, or he is on a journey, or perhaps he is asleep and must be awakened." Then they cried aloud and, as was their custom, they cut themselves with swords and lances until the blood gushed out over them. As midday passed, they raved on until the time of the offering of the oblation, but there was no voice, no answer, and no response.

Then Elijah said to all the people, "Come closer to me"; and all the people came closer to him. First he repaired the altar of the LORD that had been thrown down; Elijah took twelve stones, according to the number of the tribes of the sons of Jacob, to whom the word of the LORD came, saying, "Israel shall be your name"; with the stones he built an altar in the name of the LORD. Then he made a trench around the altar, large enough to contain two measures of seed. Next he put the wood in order, cut the bull in pieces, and laid it on the wood. He said, "Fill four jars with water and pour it on the burnt offering and on the wood." Then he said, "Do it a second time"; and they did it a second time. Again he said, "Do it a third time"; and they did it a third time, so that the water ran all around the altar, and filled the trench also with water.

At the time of the offering of the oblation, the prophet Elijah came near and said, "O LORD, God of Abraham, Isaac and Israel, let it be known this day that you are God in Israel, that I am your servant, and that I have done all these things at your bidding. Answer me, O LORD, answer me, so that this people may know that you, O LORD, are God, and that you have turned their hearts back." (1 Kgs 18:22–37)

ACCEPTING THE RIVER JORDAN OF OUR LIFE

Humor opens a space for surprise in our lives. We laugh because, unexpectedly, we come across a delightful word. In fact, the faith itself is not entirely a foreseeable experience, a fully detailed map, but rather an opening to the surprise of God, to the unlooked-for of God who is calling us. When Naaman, one of the Aramean king's generals, came to Israel and the prophet Elisha, Elijah's successor, sent him to wash seven times in the insignificant river Jordan, Naaman said:

> "I thought that for me he would surely come out, and stand and call on the name of the LORD his God, and would wave his hand over the spot, and cure the leprosy! Are not Abana and Pharpar, the rivers of Damascus, better than all the waters of Israel? Could I not wash in them, and be clean?" He turned and went away in a rage. But his servants approached and said to him, "Father, if the prophet had commanded you to do something difficult, would you not have done it? How much more, when all he said to you was, 'Wash, and be clean'?" So he went down and immersed himself seven times in the Jordan, according to the word of the man of God; his flesh was restored like the flesh of a young boy, and he was clean. (2 Kgs 5:11–14)

Laughter and joy are the easy way. When we are looking for the heroic way and striving for unusual and clever schemes, humor helps us to understand that it is when we accept simplicity, the minimum, when we accept the "river Jordan in our lives" that we are cured. The greatest in the least. The more in the less.

JESUS' SENSE OF HUMOR

There is humor in the language and life of Jesus. In Luke 24, we have a very clear example of this. The two disciples of Emmaus are talking to Jesus, but they do not recognize him. They actually say to him: "Are you the only stranger in Jerusalem who does not know the things that have taken place there in these days?" (24:18). Here we already see the main irony of the situation! But a disciple, a Christian, these too are formed by the irony of God. In other words, by experiencing the fact that God takes hold of our fatalities, our irremediable situations, the things we have not finished or have lost, and smiles (!), we then set out on a deeper and more positive route than we had supposed.

On several occasions, the people tried to seize hold of Jesus and make him king. And Jesus always escapes these attempts. But there was one occasion when Jesus himself took the initiative, when he wanted to enter Jerusalem. Except that he did it in such a strange and amusing way. He mounted a donkey and entered the city and was acclaimed king, not by the authorities, but by the children and the people in the street! It is interesting to see the way in which St. John describes all this in 12:12–16, where he tells us that "his disciples did not understand these things at first." How could one understand what had happened without entering into Jesus' prophetic sense of humor? We are reminded of the various *Christs* painted by Rouault. The *Christ Clown*, in all its drama, is also humorous, an astonishing and heartfelt outburst. It is not by suffering alone that redemption is achieved. It can also come through joy.

Humor continues in the history of the Apostles. It occurs in Acts 12, when Peter is released from prison. He goes to the house where the disciples are gathered and knocks loudly on the door. A servant girl runs to answer and asks who's there. She hears him say, "It's Peter." She recognizes his voice and hurries to tell the others that Peter is at the door. But instead of letting him in, they have a discussion. Could it be Peter? Is he not in prison? "Meanwhile, Peter continued knocking" (12:16)!

CREATION IS GOD'S DANCE

To speak of God's sense of humor in the Bible is to throw light on our condition of *homo ludens* and *homo festivus*. Amusement, good humor, and games open new doors within us! They are important means of overcoming the deadly disease of anxiety.

Good humor in the experience of faith helps us in this process of inner recreation. The experience of faith is an experience of creation and re-creation! The most powerful metaphor that St. Paul uses in speaking of Jesus Christ is this: "In him we are created and re-created" (Rom 6:8; 2 Tim 2:11). The great topic of Christian experience is this experience of being born and reborn, of a life that is open, in the process of being remade from the grace of the Spirit. The writer Flannery O'Connor, who had a wonderful sense of humor, criticized the tremendous lack of imagination in the Catholicism of her day. If we set to one side our imagination, our sense of humor, our playfulness, we end up forgetting the art of rediscovering joy. The theologian Hugo Rahner stresses that in the biblical Book of Proverbs, when it mentions God's activity, his doing and creating, the same word is used as appears in the second Book of Samuel (6:5) to describe David's dance before the Ark of the Covenant. God's work of Creation is a dance, a festive dance. It is the same word: God dances; God creates. The Creation is God's Dance. That marvelous circle of saints that Fra Angelico depicted in among the angel musicians and all with hands joined is an image that is much closer to the biblical tradition than we might have supposed. A lovely line of poetry by Auden goes like this: "I know nothing except what everyone knows—if there when Grace dances, I should dance."

16

PAUL, MASTER OF CHRISTIAN JOY

The category of "joy" deeply marks the theology of St. Paul, to the point of his claiming for himself the title of "apostle of joy." In fact, this is a constant throughout all his letters. It appears in many of the Apostle's central passages of reflection as a permanent state that must accompany the very condition of a Christian. Of the 326 times that the word *joy* appears in the New Testament, over one-third—131—occur in the writings of St. Paul.

As we shall see, joy is also linked with concrete situations, and with the amazing resonance that these have in Paul's personality. Joy has this prerogative, that of summoning us to reality and constituting a kind of barometer for indicating the state of our inner health. But in Paul's view, this happens because Christian joy exists in a close relationship with the principal axes of the *Kerygma* itself.

JOY AND THE MYSTERY OF CHRIST

Explicitly and implicitly, St. Paul's proclamation of joy is linked with the Lord's resurrection, as we see as early as in 1 Thessalonians 1:6–10, but also in other passages (cf. 2 Cor 7:3–4; 13:1–11; Phil 1:15–20; 2:17). In 1 Thessalonians, the Apostle writes:

And you became imitators of us and of the Lord, for in spite of persecution you received the word with joy inspired by the Holy Spirit, so that you became an example to all the believers in Macedonia and in Achaia. For the word of the Lord has sounded forth from you not only in Macedonia and Achaia, but in every place your faith in God has become known, so that we have no need to speak about it. For the people of those regions report about us what kind of welcome we had among you, and how you turned to God from idols, to serve a living and true God, and to wait for his Son from heaven, whom he raised from the dead—Jesus. (1:6–10)

The passage gravitates around the Word of the Lord, which is a source of joy in the life of the Apostle and of the community that imitates him. But to welcome the Word is essentially to welcome the event that the Word announces and that gives it a specific identity. In this context, we perceive the double meaning that Paul gives to the expression: "Word of the Lord"; it is Word of the Lord because it is the Risen One himself who speaks (2 Cor 13:5) and it is Word of the Lord because the Risen One is the object of the announcement (2 Cor 13:3). Hence, the outburst of joy that bubbles inevitably from this encounter of the believer with the Risen One by the power of his Word.

In the same way, the persistence of joy in the midst of sufferings and tribulations is understood to be an acceptance of the gospel of the Risen One who is also the Crucified One. Trials become precisely the circumstance in which to be mysteriously united with the Crucified Lord. There is a marvelous crescendo in the narrative of the Letters in which the glowing and hidden link between the life of the Master and the disciple, between the Lord dead and risen and the Apostle called to a death-with and a resurrection-with. This is how Paul himself links his own frailty—"We rejoice when we are weak" (2 Cor

13:9)—with the frailty of the One who first "was crucified in weakness, but lives by the power of God" (2 Cor 13:4). The possibility of joy, for Paul, rests above all on the possibility of sharing intimately and fully in the destiny of Christ. It is this that he writes in Philippians 2:17–18 where he makes use of the language of sacrifice and worship: "But even if I am being poured out as a libation over the sacrifice and the offering of your faith, I am glad and rejoice with all of you—and in the same way you also must be glad and rejoice with me."

As a synthesis and culminating point of this relationship between joy and the mystery of Christ, let us reflect on the expression "in the Lord" in Philippians 4:4: "Rejoice in the Lord always; again I will say, Rejoice!" What does this little preposition tell us? That joy does not appear as an extrinsic attachment, but implies communion, plunging one's whole being "into the Lord," and remaining there, rooted, molded, hidden, "buried" as Paul himself says at one point. "Rejoice in the Lord" is not any old enthusiastic vibration, but a recognition of the definitive nature of the resurrection over and above all other happenings and above the whole of one's life. Nothing is left out.

Very perceptively, attention has been drawn to the parallelism between the expressions "Rejoice in the Lord" in Philippians 3:1a, and "be of the same mind in the Lord" in Philippians 4:2. This second expression throws light on the underlying construction, because as yet not everything has been done. It is a tendency toward, a becoming, a following. In fact, there is a distance to be covered between what happened once and for all in the life of Jesus and what has yet to be patiently accomplished in the life of the Apostle. Paul declares expressly that Christ will be glorified in his own body: "Christ will be exalted now as always in my body, whether by life or by death" (Phil 1:20); that is, in us Christ is in the process of expanding. Concerning joy, we can therefore say that in Paul the key to it remains christological: Pauline joy is a consequence of the inauguration of the definitive act which, through the Risen One, provides both meaning and a horizon. Hence the glowing declaration: "I am filled with consolation; I am overjoyed" (2 Cor 7:4).

JOY AND THE HOLY SPIRIT

In Paul's writings, there is a surprising analogy between the Christ/joy and Spirit/joy relationship. Christian joy is also the breath of this Spirit that is a manifestation and power of God, and that possesses a fundamental continuity with Christ. It is the same joy we find in the loving attitude of the Father, in the state of the Risen One, and in the molding and transforming essence of the Spirit. In this connection, we perceive that Paul attributes to the Spirit the gift of joy. In 1 Thessalonians 1:6, Paul speaks of the "joy inspired by the Holy Spirit," and in Galatians 5:22, joy embraces—secondarily—the group of gifts that are "fruits of the Spirit." Joy is the activity released by the Spirit in the Christian's current conditions. It is exposed to the alternations of history with its tribulations and dramatic moments, but is deeply rooted in the all-transforming presence of Christ and his Spirit. But for this to be so, it has to follow a route that the Spirit points out to us with the novelty of the resurrection: "Live by the Spirit, I say" (Gal 5:16). Let yourselves be "led by the Spirit" (Gal 5:18).

This gives us St. Paul's delightful expression in Romans 14:17: "For the kingdom of God is not food and drink but righteousness and peace and joy in the Holy Spirit." It is in the sequence—righteousness, peace, and joy in the Spirit—that the kingdom of God is formed. The fact that people can say "justice and peace" is because they perceive that they reveal the kingdom, because they compel a social conversion, an effective commitment in the transformation of history. But is it plausible to include joy in this triad? Joy is a fundamental breathing in and out of the Spirit. The Spirit is the great inspirer of novelty, of renewal, of the unforeseen bubbling forth of the gift, of the old and the new charisms. It is very much responsible for the creativity of charity. Joy is the dialect, the diction, the calligraphy of the Spirit.

JOY AND THE ECCLESIAL COMMUNITY

Joy is a gift of the Spirit (see Gal 5:22), but it becomes concrete in the Apostle's encounter with the community. The community is the reason for joy. The following expressions point in this direction:

> "Yes, you are our glory and joy!" (1 Thess 2:20)
> "My brothers and sisters, whom I love and long for,
> my joy and crown." (Phil 4:1)

There is continuity between the presence of the Risen Lord and his becoming visible in the concrete density of a community. Paul's joy is the effect of what Christ accomplished for him and is palpable in the common life of all.

Paul cannot not rejoice over the fact that the Christ event has transformed the community: "Your obedience is known to all" (Rom 16:19). Not only is the gospel preached to the community, but Paul recognizes that it plays an active role in both witness and mission, in the way it both collaborates and is co-responsible: "I thank my God every time I remember you, constantly praying with joy in every one of my prayers for all of you, because of your sharing in the gospel" (Phil 1:3–5). All this provides Paul with a range of expressions that make clear the closeness of the relationship between himself and the community, manifested in bonds of real affection.

> As for us, brothers and sisters, when, for a short time, we were made orphans by being separated from you—in person, not in heart—we longed with great eagerness to see you face to face. (1 Thess 2:17)

I speak as to children—open wide your hearts also. (2 Cor 6:13)

The desire to see someone's face again is a desire for a new friendship that springs from the bond of faith, and at the same time a desire to promote greater maturity in the same faith: "We sent Timothy, our brother and co-worker for God in proclaiming the gospel of Christ, to strengthen and encourage you for the sake of your faith" (1 Thess 3:2).

With this, the difficulties and accidents that characterize this joyful relationship are not ignored. Paul is concerned with the community; he both expresses his approval and at the same time suffers. The overriding attitude never ceases to be that of joy, but in this context, Paul is also ready to accept both the difficulties and the tribulations: "We rejoice when we are weak and you are strong" (2 Cor 13:9).

The Apostle is sometimes obliged to raise his voice in order to warn the community: his responsibility for it obliges him to watch and to intervene while at the same time making it clear that the aim is the joy of conversion: "For even if I made you sorry with my letter, I do not regret it (though I did regret it, for I see that I grieved you with that letter, though only briefly). Now I rejoice, not because you were grieved, but because your grief led to repentance" (2 Cor 7:8–9).

On the other hand, there is a community joy that originates in Paul himself. He realizes that he brings joy to the community. In 2 Corinthians 1:24, we read: "We are workers with you for your joy"; and before that, when he wants to justify his not going to Corinth, he says: "Since I was sure of this, I wanted to come to you first, so that you might have a double favor" (2 Cor 1:15).

A visit from Paul is joy for the community. It is clear that this refers to a grateful acknowledgment on the part of the community. The community rejoices because of the visit, or looks forward to it because a visit from the Apostle is a sign of a visit from Christ himself. And if Paul accepts this recognition of his apostolic ministry, he extends the meaning in relation to all the members of the community. It is the same with the welcome of Titus by the community in Corinth (2 Cor 7:13): "In this we find comfort. In addition to our own consolation, we rejoiced still more at the joy of Titus." It is the same, too, in the case of the return of Epaphroditus to the community in Philippi:

> Still, I think it necessary to send to you Epaphroditus—my brother and co-worker and fellow soldier, your messenger and minister to my need; for he has been longing for all of you, and has been distressed because you heard that he was ill. He was indeed so ill that he nearly died. But God had mercy on him, and not only on him but on me also, so that I would not have one sorrow after another. I am the more eager to send him, therefore, in order that you may rejoice at seeing him again, and that I may be less anxious. Welcome him then in the Lord with all joy, and honor such people, because he came close to death for the work of Christ, risking his life to make up for those services that you could not give me. (Phil 2:25–30)

The same joy applies to all relationships. Joy and charity become one and the same in the life of the community. Joy can only be complete if the charity is lived in the whole community: "Make my joy complete: be of the same mind, having the same love, being in full accord and of one mind" (Phil 2:2). This means that this joy must be incarnate in the inner workings of charity and that these are transformed into the vital context of joy.

One text restores this Apostle-community polarity to unity, Philippians 1:25–26: "Since I am convinced of this, I know that I will remain and continue with all of you for your progress and joy in faith, so that I may share abundantly in your boasting in Christ Jesus when I come to you again." What is in question is "joy in the faith," which links the destiny of the Apostle inseparably with the life of the community. It is not a question here of the people's joy but of their *pistis*. We are dealing with a common journey, a mutual growth of which the point of convergence is Jesus Christ himself.

THE WAY OF JOY

Even though Paul does not offer an exhaustive analysis of the Christian, one can detect, especially in the parenetic sections, the place that joy is called upon to occupy in the life of a Christian. The following concluding ideas may help us to clarify the link between joy and the particular episodes, whether joyful or not, that occur in the course of a human life.

1. A particularly significant binomial is the one linking hope and joy. Let us reflect on two expressions in the Letter to the Romans: "Rejoice in hope" (12:12); and "May the God of hope fill you with all joy" (15:13). The exhortation to joy is designed to lead the Christian and the community beyond contingent situations to that bedrock of serenity that is rooted in the certain hope of all who know that, henceforth, through the mystery of Christ, a person's life is immersed in God himself. St. Paul does not invite people to indifference or to impassibility in the face of the crises and conflicts of life, but rather to that supremely decisive factor: the event of the Risen One on which they are called to construct, faithfully and creatively, their entire Christian existence.

2. But Paul also speaks—and here we have a second binomial—of a balance between the fundamental joy to which a Christian is called and the events of a life. The conception that Paul has of the communities (and of himself!) is in no way

idealized. He knows how close to each other frailty and uncertainty can be. For this very reason, he suggests two attitudes:

a. Share one another's feelings: "Rejoice with those who rejoice, weep with those who weep" (Rom 12:15). This kind of presence continues the welcome and sharing of Christ himself when he took on our humanity.

b. Weep, rejoice, and possess as if we neither wept, rejoiced, or possessed: "Those who mourn as though they were not mourning, and those who rejoice as though they were not rejoicing, and those who buy as though they had no possessions" (1 Cor 7:30).

Genuine Joy is not the euphoria of a moment but the inextinguishable and living horizon of Christ. In this sense, joy is inclusive. The lives of Christians must be in harmony with all that happened in the human life of Jesus. It becomes a eucharistic life.

Joy can then link up with prayer and thanksgiving, because it is an eschatological gift of God: "How can we thank God enough for you in return for all the joy that we feel before our God because of you?" (1 Thess 3:9); "See that none of you repays evil for evil, but always seek to do good to one another and to all. Rejoice always, pray without ceasing, give thanks in all circumstances; for this is the will of God in Christ Jesus for you" (5:15–18).

3. Paul is sometimes accused of pessimism, but Paul is only pessimistic when he is speaking of the "old man" who, embroiled in the contingencies of life, is unable to enter into an authentic state of joy. In fact, the Pauline vision seeks a particular wavelength for human existence. The contin-

gencies of life change, today it is this, tomorrow something else: night and day, joy and sorrow alternate and intersect. Everything seems precarious and relative. However, the space in which Paul moves gives absolute priority to that gift, the Spirit, which God offers unconditionally in Jesus Christ to all human beings. The Spirit of divine childhood given, in time, for all eternity. For each man and woman this is the true possibility of living joyfully; to be already loved eternally by God in Christ Jesus, to be destined for the fullness of divine childhood.

There is in fact an etymological and semantic relationship between the terms *Karâ*, which means "joy" and *Kâris*, which means "grace." Only because people are in grace can they also experience joy. Joy is the almost sacramental sign of divine grace.

Although some Hebrew lines of thought that are clearly visible in some passages in the Old Testament stressed the idea that God's blessing was concretized in the material, earthly gift (children, health, prosperity), Paul does not go down that road. This is not because he does not value the benefits that may accompany a person's life (the collection, Epaphroditus' health); rather, he gives priority to the good *par excellence*, which is the richness of the gift of God.

Again, in relation to the Hellenistic tradition, Paul knew how to make the necessary distinctions. For the Greeks, to have or not have possessions was attributed to fate, and implicitly to a divine being on whose arbitrary decision the various human situations depended. The various philosophies had endeavored to rationalize as far as possible the experience of pain and of evil and had come to a variety of conclusions: Socratic patience, Stoic peace of mind, Epicurean delight in pleasure. Paul is on another plane. There is no place for a fate that discriminates between people, or for pure human voluntarism as a solution. On the contrary, there is an invitation to joy. What happened in Jesus Christ makes all human beings "graces." It is a grace in which the Father addresses himself as Mercy to all his children, without either preference or discrimination. We thus see that joy becomes a concrete horizon in which we can perceive the originality reflected in Paul's thinking.

JOY AND ESCHATOLOGY

The first thing to remember is that joy itself is an eschatological gift: it points, in the present, to Christian fullness. Paul does not situate joy in a future of some kind, though he does in fact situate its fullness there. Joy contains the dynamic of promise. Paul speaks of tending toward perfection (2 Cor 13:11) and of "completing my joy" (Phil 2:2) expressions that speak of the growth and maturing of this joy. Joy will appear in all its intensity "before our Lord" in the Parousia (1 Thess 2:19) and before God (1 Thess 3:13). Then the promise will be completely fulfilled. This condition takes nothing away from joy, but makes clear its itinerant nature.

From this point of view, Paul's expressions that decline joy in the present and the future are interesting: "In that I rejoice. Yes, and I will continue to rejoice" (Phil 1:18), or expressing his wish for a fullness of joy and peace in the Church, as in Romans 15:13: "May the God of hope fill you with all joy and peace."

17

THE BOY, THE ANGEL, AND THE DOG

Friendship is a narrative. Hence it is not surprising that, in order to speak of it, the Bible so frequently has recourse to stories. In fact, stories are the language in which friendship is best expressed because they lay before us the landscape of the present and the concrete. Friendship is an eminently practical wisdom. One of the loveliest representations of friendship presented in the Bible is in the Book of Tobit. Tobit was a just and pious man who had pity on all his fellow citizens. One day he prepared a feast in his house and he said to his son Tobias: "Go, my child, and bring whatever poor person you may find of our people....I will wait for you." The son went to look for a poor man, and found one lying dead in the market place. Tobit immediately got up and went to bury the man. He then washed himself and mourned for him. When he returned home, the feast was no longer the same; nothing about him retained the same glow, none of the food tasted as it might have. He remembered the words of the prophet, "Your festivals shall be turned into mourning," and he felt that, on that night, his life was approaching a transformation (Tob 2:2–6).

Not long afterward, Tobias was resting with his eyes open and did not realize that there were some sparrows on top of the wall. Their fresh droppings fell into his open eyes and he became blind. He sought the help of doctors, but to no avail. Because of his blindness, the family quickly became poor. Then Tobit remembered that he had left some money in trust with a moneylender, and that he needed it now. Unfortunately, however, the moneylender lived in Media, which was a long way from the place where Tobit himself lived. His only son was the only person he could send on his behalf, but the son would need a traveling companion on such a journey. In Tobit 5:1–3, we read:

> Then Tobias answered his father Tobit, "I will do everything that you have commanded me, father; but how can I obtain the money from him, since he does not know me and I do not know him? What evidence am I to give him so that he will recognize and trust me, and give me the money? Also, I do not know the roads to Media, or how to get there." Then Tobit answered his son Tobias, "I will give you a document which he gave me. All you need do is to show it to him, and he will give you the money at once. So now, my son, find yourself a trustworthy man to go with you."

So Tobias went out to look for a man who knew the way to go with him to Media. Outside he found Raphael the angel standing in front of him (though he did not realize he was an angel of God). The Letter to the Hebrews assures us "some have entertained angels without knowing it" (Heb 13:2). Friendship is the place for such encounters. Tobit blessed the journey, saying: "'May God in heaven protect you abroad and may his angel go with you and protect you.'…The young man went out and the angel went with him; and the dog came out with him and went along with them." When they eventually returned, they were to bring the miracle with them. The image of these three setting off together is one of the most beautiful icons of friendship.

"A TREE-TOAD IS A CHEF-D'OEUVRE FOR THE HIGHEST"

There is a poem by Adília Lopes about an angel that is filled with spiritual wisdom. It goes like this:

Um anjo está contigo quando desanimas
Um anjo está contigo quando te alegras
Sempre um anjo está contigo
E o arco-íris brilha como a água que corre

An angel is by your side when you lack courage
An angel is by your side when you rejoice
There is always an angel by your side
And the rainbow glistens like running water.

But since we are reflecting on friendship, we must not forget the dog trotting along beside Tobias, for he represents the bond of friendship between human beings and all other creatures. In fact, God did not establish human beings as lords of creation but as its shepherds. Alongside many other mysteries, we are all part of a single landscape. Our task is not to dominate, but rather to be nourished by what, in such audible and yet silent ways, the other species, our companions in the great journey of the world, are saying. From this point of view, how illuminating is the truth contained in Walt Whitman's poem "Song of Myself" from *Leaves of Grass*.

I believe a leaf of grass is no less than the journey work
    of the stars,
And the pismire is equally perfect, and a grain of sand,
    and the egg of the wren,
And the tree-toad is a chef-d'oeuvre for the highest,
And the running blackberry would adorn the parlors of
    heaven,

And the narrowest hinge in my hand puts to scorn all
   machinery,
And the cow crunching with depress'd head surpasses
   any statue,
And a mouse is miracle enough to stagger sextillions of
   infidels.

The hippopotamus that appears in the Book of Job
always comes as a surprise. It is not exactly a theological joke,
since it occurs in a work that explores very seriously the limits of human responsibility in relation to the devastating experience of evil. What first appears in the Book is Job's protest
against the evil that has fallen inexplicably on himself and his
history, a protest that includes God since, at the end of the
day, he does not exempt the just from tribulation. Later, however, there comes a moment when God starts to interrogate
Job. And in this amazing dialogue, we are faced with a type of
reasoning that could hardly be more disconcerting. Job can
think only of his own suffering and the reasoning with which
he fights in vain against God. God, however, challenges Job to
look around him and see...a hippopotamus.

Look at Behemoth,
   which I made just as I made you;
   it eats grass like an ox.
Its strength is in its loins,
   and its power in the muscles of its belly.
It makes its tail stiff like a cedar;
   the sinews of its thighs are knit together.
Its bones are tubes of bronze,
   its limbs like bars of iron.

It is the first of the great acts of God.

(Job 40:15–19)

141

God's method in this extraordinary encounter with Job is to widen his ability to see, drag him forcibly before all that is great, all for which there is no answer, showing him that if evil is an enigma that silences us, good is an even greater mystery. There is equally no possible explanation for the wonderful work of the Creator. Why then insist at all costs on discovering a solution for the problem of evil when the question of the good is deeper, vaster, and more silent?

Jesus, too, calls on us to look at things: to look at the birds of the air and the lilies of the field (Luke 12:22–34). Modern life has distanced us from friendship with nature. Urban landscapes with their concrete forests enclose life within walls, they establish us in settlements with paraphernalia that ensure levels of comfort, but for some reason we call the air we breathe "air-conditioned." "Consider the ravens… consider the lilies." We need space and wide-open fields; we need to make more wide-ranging journeys. We need to come closer to the silence of things, companion to the silence of our soul. We need the untrammeled freedom of the unfathomable hours to which the round of creation bears witness. We are living unsatisfied, sad, exhausted lives because a life that is shut in is a diminished life. We need to be redeemed by really looking at things. "Consider the ravens…consider the lilies."

CAN WE BE FRIENDS WITH A FLOWER?

I shall never forget one of the first cases that a lawyer friend of mine had to defend in court. It was the case of a woman who stole vases of flowers. It was discovered that she had no proper house of her own; she lived in a kind of dark cave that had been used for years as a shelter for animals in the harshest winters. There was no means of transport to this place. The woman used to travel as far as the end of the paved road and then make her way, on foot, by a series of lonely short cuts that she knew, to the precarious place where she lived. It was here that the police found more than one hundred stolen vases which, however, the woman had kept full of flowers.

We know so little about one another and even about ourselves. Nevertheless, friendship is a circle that widens out like the ones we made when, as children, we threw stones into the lake, for we loved to see them create ever-widening circles in the water.

Can we be friends with a flower? In the entry in Etty Hillesum's diary for July 1, 1942, we read:

> How exotic the jasmine looks! How is it possible, my God, that it is there wedged between the colourless wall behind the neighbours' house and the garage? It peeps above the smooth, dark mud-brown roof of the garage. Surrounded by that grey mud-brown darkness, it is so delicate and so dazzling, so pure, so exuberant and so fragile, a young fearless bride in a disreputable neighbourhood. I know nothing about jasmines. But there is no need. It is still possible to believe in miracles."

18

FRIEND, WHY ARE YOU HERE?

The poem "A Thank-You Note" by the Polish writer Wislawa Symborska needs to be read with irony. It begins "There is much I owe/to those I do not love," whereas one might have expected her to say "I owe so much," or "I owe everything, to those I love." But in fact, the poem deconstructs the customary image of the world: "There is much I owe/to those I do not love." It goes on:

> I don't wait for them
> from window to door.
> Almost as patient as a sun dial.
>
> Between rendezvous and letter
> no eternity passes,
> only a few days or weeks.
>
> And when seven rivers and mountains
> come between us,
> they are rivers and mountains
> well known from any map.

With the good-humored wisdom characteristic of her poetry, Symborska reveals here a mysterious truth of human emotions, namely that there is a kind of suffering that only those close to us can cause us. Obviously, embarrassment, aggressiveness, and partings can come from anywhere, but no disturbance has such an effect on us, no blow wounds us so deeply as those that come to us from a brother, a sister, or a friend.

ONLY SOMEONE WHO LOVES ME CAN BETRAY ME

There is a well-known aphorism by T. E. Lawrence: "My name is for my friends. My name is for my friends." In fact, only those who love us pronounce our names correctly, know what they really mean, and are ready to articulate our world in all its complexity and enigmatic fullness. Only those who love us are capable of seeing us as we really are: this passionate and contradictory mixture, this adventure that has both reached its completion and yet is still incomplete, this bundle of nerves and soul, of opacity and glimpses of light. A poet has rightly written. "If I am not given Love, I am given nothing." Only those who love us plant in the deep earth of our heart a seed of goodness, a fragment of tomorrow. Yet, just as the night, at a certain moment, awaits the certain coming of the day, or as the storm bursts forth from balmy weather we know not how, so it is with friendship. There can come a moment, a time of life, a situation in which, to a greater or lesser extent, we feel, with a shudder, the touch of a gesture or a word that betrays us.

The sensation of having been betrayed is not just a wound; it is a crater, a cleft that tears us open from top to bottom. We thought we were living a stable history of confidence, we put all we had into it, and then we perceive that we were mistaken. Everything is out of joint. Betrayal shatters our inner picture, plunges us into disillusionment, and binds us in a widespread and unknown pain. It is true that we must ask ourselves whether our disillusionments are not due mostly to a narcissistic view of friendship or a comfortable projection of expectations onto the other, not all of which are either legitimate or sensible. We must be alert to the illusory nature of those affective relationships that merely seek a resonance of the ego and its demands. Nonetheless, even this necessary process of analysis, which normally takes time and needs the advice of others to unravel, does not do away with the harsh truth, so often spelt out in traumatic circumstances: only someone who loves me can betray me.

THE STORY OF JUDAS, FRIEND OF JESUS

Only someone who loves me can betray me: this statement, on its own, is a scandal that is difficult to accept. It costs a lot to look at it fairly and squarely, as what it says throws us off balance. It may well be this that explains, for instance, the success of modified versions of what is probably the most telling story of the betrayal of a friend, namely that perpetrated by Judas. Even very recently, the re-edition of an ancient Gnostic text entitled *The Gospel of Judas* by Simon Mawer sparked off this debate once again. Instead of being a traitor, Judas is described as an obedient disciple, faithfully carrying out an order given to him by Jesus himself, who needed such a collaborator in order to achieve his plan for salvation. Without Judas's betrayal, Jesus would not have attained his Passover. For this reason, Jesus himself persuaded Judas to betray him: "Lift up your eyes and look at the cloud and the light within it and the stars surrounding it. The star that leads the way is your star." We find the same idea in the well-known novel by Nikos Kazantzakis, *The Last Temptation of Christ* (1951). According to the author, Judas's betrayal should not been seen as such, but as a necessary step in the revelation of the Savior. "We **two must** save the world. Help me," is Jesus' strange request to Judas. These fictional ways circumvent the scandal we are talking about. We shall have other ways.

Judas is mentioned for the first time in the list of the twelve disciples that Jesus chooses to be with him (Mark 3:13–19; Matt 10:1–4; Luke 6:12–16). In Hebrew, Judas means "the beloved/the favored one," as Cephas (Peter's name) means "rock." Some scholars have seen in this signs of Jesus' sense of humor, calling "rocky" a timorous follower such as Peter and having as the disciple who betrayed him someone named "the favored one." But, even without any reference to Jesus' sense of humor (so marvelously explicit), we have to say that, in both cases, the truth of love more than prevails over the irony. There is no doubt about it: Jesus chose Judas for love and for no other reason.

As for the origin of the name Iscariot, there are two explanations for this too, which may shed some light on the person of Judas himself. The most conventional explanation makes of Judas the "man from Kerioth" (*Ish-Keriyyot*), a small village in Judea, near Hebron, which is mentioned twice in the Scriptures (Josh 15:25; Amos 2:2). It may well be that the prefix *Ish*, which means "man" in Hebrew, is here used to emphasize his social importance. If so, it would perhaps be better to translate *Iscariot* as "a gentleman from Kerioth," thus drawing attention to his prominent status. This place of origin underlines the important fact that Judas was the only disciple who was a native of Judea; all the others were Galileans. The name "beloved" is not applied to him for nothing.

The second explanation draws a parallel between the term *Iscariot* and "hired assassin,"[1] one of the titles applied to the Zealots, a group of extremely nationalistic Jews who waged armed insurrection against the Romans. In this case, Judas would have belonged to a Zealot faction before becoming a follower of Jesus and would have brought with him this dream of a political liberation, a dream that would have colored his interpretation of the path followed by Jesus.

Only someone who loves me can betray me. When we

1. Translator's note: *sicário* in Portuguese.

read the Gospels, it is impossible not to become aware of the fascination that the person and message of Jesus aroused in people. Inspired by these, Oscar Wilde offers this testimony in his "De profundis":

> I see no difficulty at all in believing that such was the charm of his personality that his mere presence could bring peace to souls in anguish, and that those who touched his garments or his hands forgot their pain; or that as he passed by on the highway of life people who had seen nothing of life's mystery, saw it clearly;...or that when he taught on the hillside the multitude forgot their hunger and thirst and the cares of this world, and that to his friends who listened to him as he sat at meat the coarse food seemed delicate, and the water had the taste of good wine, and the whole house became full of the odour and sweetness of nard.

But, alongside this enthusiasm, Jesus encountered implacable opposition, traps of all kinds laid for him, and even attempts on his life, such as happened in the synagogue in his own home town of Nazareth, as recorded by St. Luke: "When they heard this, all in the synagogue were filled with rage. They got up, drove him out of the town, and led him to the brow of the hill on which their town was built, so that they might hurl him off the cliff" (Luke 4:28–29). But, the Gospel text goes on, "he passed through the midst of them and went on his way" (4:30). In fact, those who were against him never succeeded in laying hands on Jesus or catching him in one of their traps. On the contrary, their traps turned against themselves and they began to fear the people who regarded him as a prophet (Matt 21:46). In fact, they needed a friend ready to betray him.

WHAT DOES THE WORD *FRIEND* MEAN?

Judas's betrayal is described directly and impressively, as we shall see, but perhaps the most painful aspect of the account is the fact that a symbol of friendship is used to accomplish it. A kiss on the cheek was the custom between friends, as it still is today. In a relationship between master and disciple, the kissing of hands would be customary as a sign of respect. However, Jesus is an unusual Master, even in the way in which he treated his disciples. This is clear in the episode of the washing of the feet, the unusualness of which is clearly underlined by Peter's astonished reaction: "Lord, are you going to wash my feet?" (John 13:6). Therefore, it is not odd that Judas kisses his master, Jesus. The real surprise is that Jesus, knowing the meaning of that kiss, still calls him "friend."

By that act, Judas reveals that he is no longer Jesus' friend. Jesus, however, calls him "friend" not only before but during the very act of betrayal. It is as if Jesus' friendship was to the end and beyond the end. Even though by this violent rupture Judas reveals his failure to understand Jesus, Jesus continues to be faithful to him. We learned in our schoolbooks of the famous aphorism attributed to the Roman proconsul Servilius Caepio: "Rome does not pay traitors" (*Roma traditoribus non premia*). Jesus, however, calls him friend. What does the word *friend* mean? Rainer Maria Rilke wrote, "Almost everything that happens is unrepeatable and it happens in a space that no word has ever entered." What does the word *friend* mean? I think of the words of Leif Kristiansson: "One is never really alone when one has a friend. A friend hears what you say and tries to understand what you do not know how to say." In the difficult encounter between friends, Jesus says to Judas that he is not alone, that he is listening to him, that he shares his destiny with him, that he feels he is part of Judas

149

and Judas is part of himself, that he offers him his stolen life, that he offers him life, and for this reason accepts his kiss.

THE BETRAYAL SCENE

In the three Synoptic Gospels, Jesus is betrayed by this kiss. In Mark's account, Jesus has no time to react:

> Immediately, while he was still speaking, Judas, one of the twelve, arrived; and with him there was a crowd with swords and clubs, from the chief priests, the scribes, and the elders. Now the betrayer had given them a sign, saying, "The one I will kiss is the man; arrest him and lead him away under guard." So when he came, he went up to him at once and said, "Rabbi!" and kissed him. Then they laid hands on him and arrested him. (14:43–46)

In Matthew's account, the agonized (and fertile) question reverberates: "Friend, why are you here?"

> While he was still speaking, Judas came, one of the twelve, and with him a great crowd with swords and clubs, from the chief priests and the elders of the people. Now the betrayer had given them a sign, saying, "The one I shall kiss is the man; seize him." And he came up to Jesus at once and said, "Hail, Master!" And he kissed him. Jesus said to him, "Friend, why are you here?" Then they came up and laid hands on Jesus and seized him. (26:47–50, RSV)

In Luke, we have a new element: indignation at the fact of the betrayal having been performed by means of a kiss, yes, a kiss! It is as if the fact of this unheard-of manipulation of the grammar used to express friendship and affection had doubled the scandal involved. "Judas, one of the twelve, was leading them. He approached Jesus to kiss him; but Jesus said to him, 'Judas, is it with a kiss that you are betraying the Son of Man?'" (22:47–48).

JUDAS'S MOTIVES

Why did Judas betray Jesus?

When he began to follow Jesus, he was undoubtedly full of idealism, conviction, and truth. The writer Paul Claudel puts the following words into his mouth:

> It cannot be said that in me there was what people call a flash in the pan. Nor was it a youthful enthusiasm that got hold of me, nor a feeling I can't quite describe unless I call it "sentimental." It was something absolutely serious, a deep interest. I wanted to see things clearly, I wanted to know where He was going.

We can believe that, to begin with, there was this longing for a deeper knowledge, "to know where He was going." The desire to see with his own eyes, to become involved, was genuine. Later on, dust began to accumulate, embarrassing situations, standoffs, differences of outlook. And so we enter into the discussion of the historical reasons, of which there are always many, ranging from character defects to fixed convictions. But there is more. The Gospel accounts themselves, which reflect a great deal on the case of Judas, also endeavor to read it as an expression of the drama that confronts us with the mystery of evil.

It is in the Gospel of John that we learn that Judas was responsible for administering the goods of the group, and that the others came to suspect that he was less than honest:

> Six days before the Passover Jesus came to Bethany, the home of Lazarus, whom he had raised from the dead. There they gave a dinner for him. Martha

served, and Lazarus was one of those at the table with him. Mary took a pound of costly perfume made of pure nard, anointed Jesus' feet, and wiped them with her hair. The house was filled with the fragrance of the perfume. But Judas Iscariot, one of his disciples (the one who was about to betray him), said, "Why was this perfume not sold for three hundred denarii and the money given to the poor?" (He said this not because he cared about the poor, but because he was a thief; he kept the common purse and used to steal what was put into it.) (12:1–6)

This could be the reason: Judas, consumed with greed, used the group's common fund for his own purposes. We know how the seductive power of money can lead to many betrayals. History is full of sons who, for this reason, rebel against their fathers, brothers who fight against brothers, lifelong friends who quarrel. According to St. Matthew's account, the question that Judas asked the members of the Sanhedrin may well reveal the madness that had taken hold of him. "What will you give me if I betray him to you?" (Matt 26:15). The Sanhedrin gave him thirty pieces of silver, the equivalent of 120 denarii in Roman money, the price of a slave as prescribed by the law.

But Judas may have acted as a "seeker after justice" for ideological reasons rather than greed for gold. Like the rest of the disciples, he was convinced that Jesus was on his way to Jerusalem in order to establish the kingdom of God and the *Verus Israel* in the form of a political power, so much so that they discussed among themselves which place each of them would occupy there (Luke 9:46; Mark 10:34–40). This expectation was raised by the means Jesus chose to enter Jerusalem: mounted on a donkey, as foretold by the prophet Zechariah: "Lo, your king comes to you…humble and riding on a donkey" (Zech 9:9), and accompanied by the messianic shouts of the crowd: "Blessed is the one who comes in the name of the Lord" (Matt 21:9).

But as time went by, the way Jesus behaved in Jerusalem was determinedly antitriumphal. He refused to say "by what authority" he was acting (Luke 20:8); he avoided performing miracles and contented himself with merely preaching. Now the disciples themselves and the people as a whole had seen much more than this from Jesus in Galilee, so now they felt that their expectations had been *betrayed*. According to the hypothesis that Judas was a Zealot, on fire with nationalist ideals, we can suppose that he took Jesus' attitude in Jerusalem rather badly. Clearly moving away from the political Messianism that surrounded him, Jesus became a doubt in Judas's heart: if he did not match the idea that one looked for in a Messiah, could he in fact be the Messiah? Might it not all have been a foolish mistake? In the end, Judas became a traitor because he himself felt betrayed. It is this betrayal that prompts him to act. It is very clear from the way things worked out that everything was decided during the Last Supper as far as he was concerned. When, as Jesus broke and shared out the bread, he announced that he was willing to accept his death as a gift, Judas felt this was intolerable. He did not want a Messiah who died. He got up and left the room. In a comment that goes well beyond mere chronology, John's Gospel states: "And it was night" (John 13:30).

GOING OUT INTO THE NIGHT

The Gospel texts speak of this night. St. John says, "The devil had already put it into the heart of Judas son of Simon Iscariot to betray him" (John 13:2). Similarly, we read in St. Luke, "Satan entered into Judas called Iscariot, who was one of the twelve" (22:3). The night into which the act of betrayal thrusts us is the mystery of evil. It is a night of radical inner turmoil, of the overthrow of the subject, of the confused invasion of darkness that turns each one of us into the plaything of destructive passions. The texts describe it soberly without going into detail. They state quite simply that such a night exists, that it knocks us off our feet like an avalanche and that, while remaining responsible for our own actions, we forget what we are in what we do. As Fernando Pessoa wrote at the beginning of *The Book of Disquiet*, "The human soul is an obscure abyss....However much we take off what we are wearing, we will never be naked because nakedness is a phenomenon of the soul and not merely of undressing....All that we are is what we are not."

In attempting to draw a map of the act of betrayal, we are led to reflect on its triadic structure. The person who betrays lives a double "belonging," falsifying and being false to, in an unsustainable position between two conflicting truths. To betray is to remain of set purpose in this ambiguous set-up, in the position of advantage it is supposed to offer, in which no truth remains stable, and a generalized relativism wins out over the savor of opportunisms. As Jesus said, "No one can serve two masters; for a slave will either hate the one and love the other, or be devoted to the one and despise the other" (Matt 6:24). At times, we find ourselves in this situation. As Pope Benedict XVI has said, "In effect, the possibilities to pervert the human heart are truly many. The only way to prevent it consists in not cultivating an individualistic, autonomous vision of things, but on the contrary, by putting oneself always on the side of Jesus, assuming his point of view. We must daily seek to build full communion with him."

IS IT I, LORD?

I often think about that evening when Jesus, seated at table with the twelve disciples, told them that one of them was about to betray him. And they all began to ask, each one in turn: "Surely not I, Lord?" (Matt 26:22). We are tempted to attribute the ability to betray to Judas alone, placing ourselves completely outside such a picture. This is what the philosopher René Girard calls the "scapegoat" mechanism: choosing someone to carry our own violence. We make this person the alternative victim, and we load onto them everything that we ourselves dislike or that we do not wish to see in ourselves. The scapegoat is used to resolve (in fact, it serves only to postpone) our internal crises. Each of the disciples in turn asks, "Surely not I, Lord?" We ourselves need to ask the same question.

19

HAPPY GOOD THIEVES
IN PARADISE

Trust does not live on a static or caged-in image of the other. To trust is to recognize the possibility of a change, of a U-turn, of a shift in perspective and, in a sense, even of a "betrayal." Clearly, whenever a betrayal occurs, it causes surprise and hurt, precisely because it happens within the context of trust. With further reference to the friendship between Jesus and Judas, Charles Péguy wrote in *The Mystery of the Charity of Joan of Arc*,

> Being the Son of God, Jesus knew everything,
> ...And the Saviour knew that the Judas whom He
>   loved,
> He would not be able to save, though he gave himself
>   completely.
> ...It was then that Jesus experienced infinite suffering.

But to base a friendship on trust does not mean to ensure that we shall never be deceived or that we ourselves will never deceive the other. No one is exempt from this trial. In a sense, trust and betrayal constitute an expression of humanity, albeit on different moral and existential planes. Each of us needs trust, but no friendship pact is free from the turbulence of our own limitations, incoherences, and weaknesses. The experience of friendship is based on forgiveness.

The concept of betrayal is omnipresent in the life of the psyche, in each of the fundamental phases of the growth of each person to maturity. One can almost describe our development as a story in which we occupy, at times the place of betrayers, and at others that of the betrayed. We experience the first "betrayal" of all at the moment of our birth, when we are forcibly expelled from our mother's body. We are propelled out into a space where we feel unprotected, as if a bond of affection had been broken together with the umbilical cord, and will need to be put back together. The second betrayal is the so-called "oedipal betrayal" when we develop an exclusive attachment to one or other of our parents. "Who do you like best? Your Dad or your Mom?" we are asked. And we live with a sense of guilt over the reply we give (or don't give). We feel bad when we realize that we are fonder of one parent rather than the other, and are living this affinity as if the other had been eliminated symbolically. The third betrayal is that of the differentiation and independence in relation to our parents that comes about as we grow into adulthood. We feel, or we are made to feel, as if we are betraying them. As we gradually become ourselves, we also become different people, we become strangers as if we had suddenly arrived from another planet or were speaking an unknown language. We choose a political party or a sports club that is not our parents'; we develop friendships that they consider undesirable or impossible; we listen to loud music that they detest. We betray their dreams and expectations. Our personal life appears to be a betrayal whereas it is in fact quite simply life.

To leave one's native land, abandon one's former masters, change one's way of thinking and behaving. "Go…to the land that I will show you," God said to Abraham (Gen 12:1). "Come, follow me," said Jesus (Mark 10:21). "Life is a series of beginnings," commented St. Gregory the Great. In fact, we are always beginning again, making a new start. But for this reason, we cannot escape from remaining for a long time (and also painfully) on a kind of knife-edge: in our loyalty, are we really being loyal or simply conforming and toeing the line? In our "betrayals," are we really being traitors or simply making a change, in order to see better, to be precisely what we are? In exercising our personal independence, are we living out a legitimate freedom or are we indulging in ingratitude and self-ishness in relation to others? It is important to look calmly at these questions and make of them a way forward.

What happens with individuals as such happens also to the various clubs and associations to which we belong. And of course it happens with friendship as well. There are ways of sharing that run the risk of drowning in a narcissistic by-water, when they lose sight of the horizon of the universal. I have a friend who says, very wisely, that mothers who are no more than mothers of their children are not true mothers. In order to be truly father, mother, brother, sister, or friend, it is neces-sary to acquire also an absolute acceptance. Those who are true fathers or mothers to their son or daughter are ready to extend and practice their parenthood whenever necessary, welcoming, listening, supporting. Someone who is no more than a friend of his or her friend, will not, strictly speaking, make a better world. Friendship is not to be confused with an egotistical association of interests in which everything begins and ends in the claustrophobic comfort of a partnership that does not invest in amplifying our ability to be. True friendship transfigures and widens our humanity, gives us emotional skills, encourages us to open the circle, to do more, to be bet-ter. Friendship inspires us to get down off our high horse, including as regards the logic of enmity, as Jesus challenges us to do: "You have heard that it was said, 'You shall love your neighbor and hate your enemy'. But I say to you, Love your enemies and pray for those who persecute you, so that you may be children of your Father in heaven; for he makes his sun rise on the evil and on the good" (Matt 5:43–45). What kind of perfection is this? All I know is that one of the ways of imple-menting it happens to us quite simply and consists in our not blocking the ongoing movement of life. Create more open spaces than walls, make more tables than chests; open up, open out, keep on opening. It can also happen that this gesture of openness may be denounced as a betrayal of the interests of the group. But in order to be faithful to the deepest level of authenticity, we must be continually asking ourselves, "What does it mean to betray?" However, let us not forget what Kierkegaard teaches us: the only real betrayal is not to have sought deeply and authentically.

ACCEPTING THE VULNERABILITY OF GOD

We often feel as if God is betraying us. We were hoping for this or that, we prayed, we promised, and then we find our hands filled with a silence that we do not know how to read. It is true that Sacred Scripture warns us: "If we are faithless, he remains faithful—for he cannot deny himself (2 Tim 2:13). But we are not always able to welcome his silences with hope.

It is through necessity that the natural religiosity of human beings places them in the presence of the Divine: we need a God who is useful to us, who has power in the world, who protects us. God very quickly turns into an idol, which guarantees that the whole wide world will function in our favor. The Bible, however, points us in the direction of a personal God, and it does so in ways that are ever more surprising (to the extent of sometimes being scandalously surprising!). For example, the God proclaimed by Jesus Christ helps us not through a magic or providentialistic understanding of his omnipotence, but by means of his fatherhood, by the gift of his love. When, in the parable of the prodigal son, the elder brother criticizes his father for never having given him a kid with which to make merry with his friends (Luke 15:29), the father explains what he explains to ourselves at the same time: "Son, you are always with me, and all that is mine is yours" (Luke 15:31). The great challenge of Christian spirituality is located precisely here in this change of attitude, in this conversion: we have to learn to appreciate the depth and the intensity of God's presence rather than whatever it is that he gives us: "You are always with me, and all that is mine is yours." Everything turns on a gratuitous relationship, and not on one interested merely in give and take. This is the decisive difference in relation to the traditional picture of the religious phenomenon.

The true Christian vision of God presents us, as it were, with a God who is useless, a God revealed in the extreme abandonment and fragility of his Messiah. Those who were present at the crucifixion said, "He saved others; he cannot save himself. He is the King of Israel; let him come down from the cross now, and we will believe in him" (Matt 27:42). It is this inability to "save himself" that plunges us into the divine mystery revealed to us in Jesus. In a letter written in prison, the theologian Dietrich Bonhoeffer commented at length on this intuition:

> We cannot be honest unless we recognize that we have to live in a world *etsi deus non daretur* [as if God did not exist]. We have to recognize before God that the God who is with us is the God who forsakes us ("My God, my God, why hast Thou forsaken me?" Mark 15:34). The God who lets us live in the world without the working hypothesis of God is the God before whom and in whom we stand continually. The God nailed to the Cross is the God who is weak and helpless in the world. And precisely for this reason, He is the God who is with us and helps us.

There is a link with God that is the fruit of acceptance of the vulnerability in which he makes himself present in history. But once again, I repeat, it is only by means of a conversion that we come to realize this.

Can it be that God betrays his friendship with us when he seems not to fulfill our expectations? Etty Hillesum wrote as follows in her diary, one of the most inspiring spiritual texts of the twentieth century:

> But one thing is becoming increasingly clear to me: that You cannot help us but we must help You to help ourselves....Yes, my God, as for our circumstances...it is clear that they are indissolubly part of this life. Neither do I hold you responsible; it is You who may well, later on, call us to account. And, at almost every heart-beat, it becomes increasingly clear to me: that You cannot help us, but we must help you and defend your dwelling place inside us to the last (July 12, 1942).

ACCEPTING OUR TEARS

It is one thing to regard trust in a friendship as a magic yielding to the benevolence and protection of the other. But this is an inadequate stage that we are called upon to transcend. It is quite another and more spiritually adult thing to understand that vulnerability involves the dynamism of one's trust. Life is polyphonic, it is a horizon with ways in and out, many of which are incomplete and imperfect; it is a place where one may meet many people and re-meet them, where there are wounds and healings. The most solid friendships are those that accept their fragile pathways, their humble cobbling together.

Our gradual growth in confidence necessarily involves our learning to accept our tears. In this, the figure of St. Peter can function as our interior mirror. Peter, like Judas, betrayed Jesus. And, again like Judas, he repented. But Judas was unable to count on being forgiven and granted mercy. He was unable to let Jesus see his tears. Very often in a friendship it is this alone that is missing. Let us recall the page from St. Luke's Gospel:

Then they seized him and led him away, bringing him into the high priest's house. But Peter was following at a distance. When they had kindled a fire in the middle of the courtyard and sat down together, Peter sat among them. Then a servant-girl, seeing him in the firelight, stared at him and said, "This man also was with him." But he denied it, saying, "Woman, I do not know him." A little later someone else, on seeing him, said, "You also are one of them." But Peter said, "Man, I am not!" Then about an hour later still another kept insisting, "Surely this man also was with him; for he is a Galilean." But Peter said, "Man, I do not know what you are talking about!" At that moment, while he was still speaking, the cock crowed. The Lord turned and looked at Peter. Then Peter remembered the word of the Lord, how he had said to him, "Before the cock crows today, you will deny me three times." And he went out and wept bitterly. (Luke 22:54–62)

The key word that released the change in Peter's heart was the reminder of the Word of the Lord. To remember is to awaken something inside oneself possessing great symbolic significance. To remember is to embark on an inward journey. It is to return to reciprocity, place oneself once again in the presence of the other, arouse once again the sleeping depths of a true friendship. Isaac of Nineveh taught:

Blessed is the man who knows his own weakness. Blessed is the one who says: "I am an unhappy one, a wretch, a poor specimen, blind, dumb." For those who acknowledge their sins are greater than those who, by praying, bring the dead to life. Those who weep for an hour over their sins are greater than those who are at the service of the entire world.

162

Those who were judged worthy to see themselves
as they really are, are greater than those who were
allowed to see the angels.

I think of the moving painting of Peter in tears by El
Greco, a theme rarely depicted in Christian iconography prior
to the sixteenth century, and one that the painter helped to
make popular. In this representation, the feature that captures
our attention is the very human face of the repentant apostle.
Peter simply raises his eyes, a look that is both completely
open and poor like a prayer, a look that reveals his frailty with
no attempt at concealment or self-defense, a look that at last
lets him weep all his tears. But to the left of the space where
Peter is standing, in the background, El Greco has depicted
two small figures, with features that evoke the light of a dawn.
Who are these figures that are almost invisible but which are
so important for the theological reading of the scene? One of
them is Mary Magdalene who is walking toward the tomb
with a vase of perfume; the other is the angel in shining gar-
ments who has been sent to announce the resurrection. This
helps us to realize that it is Easter Sunday morning.
Magdalene is in the picture because she shares with Peter (and
with ourselves) a history of betrayal and of conversion. She is
the sinner who becomes a disciple of Jesus and who becomes
the first Easter witness. Peter and Magdalene help us to see
that, in the history of our friendship with Jesus, in the history
of all our friendships, betrayal is not strictly speaking the real
obstacle. It can even be a violent way of waking us up and so
represent the opportunity for a greater grace to mend our
heart. The obstacle is to persist in banality and mere formal-
ism, to pretend, to never get beyond the door, to live on the
surface, to be neither hot nor cold, to run away from any more
demanding commitment, to keep running away from ourselves, to prefer pretense to painful (and joyful) authenticity. *In
Tuning in to Grace*, André Louf writes, "Holiness does not lie
on the other side of temptation; it is to be found in the midst

of temptation. It does not sit waiting for us on a level above our weakness; it is given us in weakness, for only then are we close to holiness."

We learn to be better at overcoming betrayal in the course of a friendship when we seriously endeavor not to be traitors to ourselves. There is great realism in the words with which Arno Gruen begins his work entitled *The Betrayal of the Self. The Fear of Autonomy in Men and Women*: "Human development offers two alternatives, *love* and *power*. The way of power, which underlies the majority of cultures, leads to an Ego that reflects the ideology of domination. Such an Ego rests on the state of fragmentation, more concretely on that division in the Ego that rejects suffering and lack of support as signs of weakness and, at the same time, highlights power and domination as ways of denying the lack of support. The achievement that passes for success in our civilization presupposes an Ego thus constituted. This situation represents the antithesis of autonomy." We would say that it also represents the antithesis of friendship.

THIEVES HAPPY IN PARADISE

I recall two films about friendship. The stories they tell are very different. One of them is close to being a fairy tale and the other is virtually a historic document, but both can be seen as parables. They not only tell their own story, they tell our story too, expressing what our own life is or can be.

The first film is *E.T. the Extra Terrestrial*, the film produced by Steven Spielberg in 1982. It tells the story of an alien who gets lost in stellar space and becomes friends with an earthling, a little boy called Elliot. Elliot brings E.T. into his house and gradually discovers the sensitive and good-humored companion hidden behind the creature's extraordinary face. Like all friends, they both learn to laugh at little tricks, they have things just between themselves, they help each other. When E.T. is frightened by an umbrella, Elliott is shaken, stealing all the food in the refrigerator. When Mary is reading *Peter Pan* to Gertie, Elliot and E.T. listen to the story while hidden in a cupboard. When Elliot accidentally cuts his finger, E.T. heals it with his own illuminated finger. The final scene portrays a miracle such as those that friendship can produce. All possible human ways of escape are blocked and it suddenly seems that there is no way of saving E.T. from those who are after him. Then Elliot's bicycle begins to go up into space, like a comet. "I'll be right here," E.T. says, pointing to Elliot's heart. Like so many stories for children, the film makes us adults think.

The other film is the one by Xavier Beauvois, *Of Gods and Men* (2010), which helped to make available to a wide public the story of the seven Trappist monks from the Monastery of Our Lady of Mount Atlas in the tiny village of Tibhirine in Algeria. The witness that these Christian monks offer is one of friendship to the Moslem community that surrounded the monastery, and also friendship to God's future. They were captured, and later assassinated, in 1996. But the truth is that their lives had been offered up much earlier.

The Frenchman, Christian de Chergé, aged 59, was the prior of the community. He belonged to a military family; he had first known Algeria as a child and, later, during the twenty-seven months of his military service during the war of independence. During that time, something happened that was to mark his life from then on: his life was saved by a Moslem friend. He was to return to that country in 1971, but this time as a monk. And it is he who wrote, in his own name, the impressive "testament" of that small, prophetic community:

> If it should happen one day—and it could be today—that I become a victim of the terrorism which now seems ready to engulf all the foreigners living in Algeria, I would like my community, my Church and my family to remember that my life was GIVEN to God and to this country. I ask them

to accept the fact that the One Master of all life was not a stranger to this brutal departure....

I could not desire such a death. It seems to me important to state this. I do not see, in fact, how I could rejoice if the people I love were indiscriminately accused of my murder....

For me, Algeria and Islam are something different: it is a body and a soul. I have proclaimed this often enough, I think, in the light of what I have received from it. I so often find there that true strand of the Gospel which I learned at my mother's knee, my very first Church, precisely in Algeria....

For this life lost, totally mine and totally theirs, I thank God, who seems to have willed it entirely for the sake of that joy in everything and in spite of everything. In this "thank you," which is said for everything in my life from now on, I certainly include you, friends of yesterday and today, and you, my friends of this place, along with my mother and father, my sisters and brothers and their families. You are the hundredfold granted as was promised! And also you, my last-minute friend, who will not have known what you were doing: Yes, I want this "thank you" and this "goodbye" to be a "God-bless" for you, too, because in God's face I see yours. May we meet again as happy thieves in Paradise, if it please God, the Father of us both.

20

SOLITUDE AND SILENCE

The solitude that hurts is the unwelcome solitude that is brought about in most cases by an affective incommunicability. We have no one with whom to discuss our lives, to share a secret. We ourselves do not receive the stories of others. To be alone is not the same as being on one's own. All of us are alone, but to be entirely on one's own is the completion, however temporary, of a severance. We begin to be increasingly cut off in a soundproof bubble. There is a sense in which the weight of life buries us. Everything seems to us strangely uniform and valueless. It seems that nothing in the world weighs on us; and we convince ourselves that we do not need anything that might be offered to us. It is as if we had moved onto an inclined plane so that even the smallest customs that represented some hope—greeting a neighbor or a stranger, walking across the garden—become increasingly difficult and we do our best to avoid them. Clearly, an undeniable anxiety underlies this state of things. In his novel, *The Hermit*, Eugène Ionesco wrote: "For days on end, I went backward and forward, from the door to the window, from the window to the door, without being able to stop. It was not anxiety, it was boredom, a material boredom, a physical boredom. Everything meant suffering, everything was gangrene of the soul....I could not stand solitude."

The writer Paul Auster makes a curious comment on the Book of Jonah. In his opinion, that little book, the only one written in the third person, as if the "I" had mislaid itself, "is the most dramatic story of solitude in the Bible." Jonah was plunged in the darkness of solitude: first, in the bowels of the ship when he was fleeing from God; then in the belly of the whale when he was fleeing from himself. "The waters closed in over me; the deep surrounded me; weeds were wrapped around my head at the roots of the mountains. I went down to the land whose bars closed on me forever" (Jonah 2:5–7). Even so, Jonah's solitude was not absolute. He turned to God like someone who turns to a friend: "I called to the LORD out of my distress, and he answered me; out of the belly of Sheol I cried, and you heard my voice" (2:2). The story of Jonah shows how friendship is solitude brought to an end.

ROOM TO FALL AND ROOM TO GET UP AGAIN

The word *solitude* is ambiguous. It can be used to describe both an experience of the labyrinth, of humiliation and extreme isolation, and it can also be the *habitat* sought out for the purpose of a deeper encounter with oneself, with others, with God. Is not solitude itself also a doorway? Does it not happen that at times an unexpected vision occurs in the most silent isolation? In one of his poems, St. John of the Cross uses the category of "sounding solitude":

> The tranquil night
> at the time of the rising dawn,
> silent music,
> sounding solitude,
> the supper that refreshes and deepens love.
> (Stanzas 14 and 15 of *The Spiritual Canticle*)

Solitude reveals the form of the night as something heard, the night as a way of listening, and whispers to us that solitude itself is tactile, giving us access to a presence "which deepens love." St. John himself explains: "This is the sounding solitude the soul knows here; that is, the testimony to God that, in themselves, all things give. Since the soul does not receive this sonorous music without solitude and estrangement from all exterior things, it calls it 'silent music' and 'sounding solitude' which, it says, is the Beloved." Hence, solitude can provide room to fall or room to get up again.

A "PEDAGOGY OF SILENCE"

The spiritual perception of silence offered by the Bible is predominantly positive. The prophet Elijah perceives the presence of God not in the noise of the hurricane that is heard at once, but in the faint sound of a gentle breeze (see 1 Kgs 19:11–13) for which it was necessary to listen attentively. In response to God's challenge: "Ask what I should give you" (1 Kgs 3:5), Solomon replies: "Give your servant…a listening heart" (1 Kgs 3:9, NABRE). The Wisdom books make use of silence to construct a route to mystagogy (progressive entry into the mystery). Anyone who reads the Book of Ecclesiastes learns silence as prudence: There is "a time to keep silence, and a time to speak" (3:7). "Never be rash with your mouth" (5:2) is the advice given in another passage. Along the same lines, in the Book of Proverbs we read: "When words are many, transgression is not lacking, but the prudent are restrained in speech" (10:19). Job himself finally falls silent before God: "See, I am of small account; what shall I answer you? I lay my hand on my mouth. I have spoken once…but will proceed no further." (Job 40:4–5).

Jesus' silence begins with the so-called hidden life that preceded his messianic activity; it is apparent in his journeying through deserts and lonely places, particularly in the course of his passion. Jesus endures in silence the complex judicial process that condemned him, so much so that the earliest Christian texts highlighted the parallel with the person of the suffering Servant in the Book of Isaiah: "He was oppressed, and he was afflicted, yet he did not open his mouth; like a lamb that is led to the slaughter, and like a sheep that before its shearers is silent, so he did not open his mouth" (Isa 53:7). Jesus was silent before the High Priest who interrogated him (Matt 26:62–63), before Herod (Luke 23:9), and finally before Pilate (John 19:9). This is the silence of the victim, but it is also the silence of trusting self-abandonment, regardless of the evidence, against all hope. It is thus that a life of God is woven in us too.

SILENCE IN THE CHRISTIAN TRADITION

Among the Fathers of the Church, the treatment of silence by Gregory Nazianzen († 390) is outstanding. For him, silence is superior to the desert and to fasting. "You seek the desert and fasting, I seek silence." More than a form of ascesis, silence is a gift that needs to be sought after and welcomed. In a hymn for Easter Sunday that brings to an end the absolute silence that had been imposed during Lent, he sings: "Today I make my voice be heard; I open my lips which silence had sealed and You find in me a zither ready to play." Silence prepares us for the music that would not emerge without it. Toward the end of the fifth century and the beginning of the sixth, Pseudo-Dionysius, a neo-Platonic theologian and philosopher, was to elaborate the mystical dimension of silence. Let us listen to him: "We venture to deny everything in relation to God in order to attain this sublime unknowing which is hidden from us by all we know about the rest of creatures, in order to contemplate this supernatural darkness which is hidden from our eyes by the light!" Or again, "O Trinity, You who oversee the divine Christian wisdom, lead us not only beyond all light, but beyond all unknowing, to the highest peak of the mystical Scriptures, where the simple, absolute and incorruptible mysteries of the divinity are revealed in Darknesses more luminous than Silence. It is in silence, in fact, that we learn the secrets of these Darknesses…that shine more luminously in the depth of the darkest obscurity…" (*On the Divine Names and the Mystical Theology*).

We can say that the thread of silence is unbreakable even though today it seems to us inaudible. Among the Latin Fathers, St. Jerome ventures to say that one can recognize the monk by his silence, not by anything he has to say. For Ambrose, silence is indispensable if we wish "to keep the secret of the Eternal King." Augustine used to say that true prayer is the silent prayer of the heart. In his *Confessions*, there is a truly extraordinary passage, the ecstasy of Ostia, which occurs in the company of his mother, Monica. It is an exaltation of the mystical order, which imposes silence successively on the flesh, the earth, the heavens, and the soul itself in order to listen to the Word of God beyond all words (IX, 10, 23–24):

> As the day now approached on which she was to depart this life—a day which thou knewest, but which we did not—it happened (though I believe it was by thy secret ways arranged) that she and I stood alone, leaning in a certain window from which the garden of the house we occupied at Ostia at the mouth of the Tiber could be seen. Here in this place, removed from the crowd, we were resting ourselves for the voyage after the fatigues of a long journey.
>
> We were conversing alone very pleasantly and "forgetting those things which are past, and reaching forward toward those things which are future." We were in the present—and in the presence of Truth (which thou art)—discussing together what is the nature of the eternal life of the saints: which eye has not seen, nor ear heard, neither has it entered into the heart of man. We opened wide the mouth of our heart, thirsting for those supernal streams of thy fountain, "the fountain of life" which

171

is with thee, that we might be sprinkled with its waters according to our capacity and might in some measure weigh the truth of so profound a mystery. And when our conversation had brought us to the point where the very highest of physical sense and the most intense illumination of physical light seemed, in comparison with the sweetness of that life to come, not worthy of comparison, nor even of mention, we lifted ourselves with a more ardent love toward the Selfsame, and we gradually passed through all the levels of bodily objects, and even through the heaven itself, where the sun and moon and stars shine on the earth.

Indeed, we soared higher yet by an inner musing, speaking and marvelling at thy works. And we came at last to our own minds and went beyond them.... And while we were thus speaking and straining after that Wisdom, we just barely touched her with the whole effort of our hearts. Then with a sigh, leaving the first fruits of the Spirit bound to that ecstasy, we returned to the sounds of our own tongue, where the spoken word had both beginning and end. But what is like to thy Word, our Lord?" (*Confessions*, trans. Albert C. Outler)

THE SCHOOL OF SILENCE

Monastic life makes of silence a condition of existence and a necessary accompaniment for the spiritual life. "Anyone who does not seek solitude cannot be silent; anyone who is not silent cannot hear the One who speaks. May the earth of my soul be silent in your presence, Lord, so that I may hear what the Lord my God is saying within me. For the words that you whisper can only be heard in a deep silence"—we learn from the Carthusian tradition. And this applies to the knowledge of oneself, of others, and of God.

The Fathers of the Desert made silence into a culture. A religious and praying culture: Evagrius bore witness to silence as prayer: "Let your tongue pronounce no words when you begin to pray." Culture of the maturing of the subject: the advice of Arsenius was as follows: "Fly. Be silent. Keep recollected." Culture of the world: Poemen guarantees: "If you are really silent, wherever you are you will find rest." Culture of being: for three years, Agathon kept stones in his mouth, not in order to become an orator like Demosthenes, but in order to learn how to be silent. Culture of hospitality: Pambo, for example, welcomed the patriarch Theophilus without saying a single word. Later he explained: if he had not been welcomed by my silence, he would most certainly not have been by my words."

Similarly, Meister Eckhart and the Rhineland mystics, as well as mysticism right up to the present day, in many ways teach silence as meaning. Eckhart urges us to find teachers in order to learn silence, a suggestion that we can act on either as individuals or as a community:

> A person who has gained the mastery of his or her life is worth more than a thousand people who have only mastered the content of books. No one can achieve anything in life without God. If I were looking for a master of learning, I would need to go to Paris or attend the faculties which run courses in more or less higher studies. But if I were interested in perfecting my life, they would not be able to teach me anything. Where then should I go? To someone possessing a pure and free nature and nowhere else: in this person I would find the answer to the thing I am so earnestly seeking. Perfection depends entirely on accepting poverty, wretchedness, hardship, disappointments and everything else that can occur during one's life, freely, and avidly until death, as if the person had been educated for this. In silence,

without asking why. (Raymond Blakney, *Meister Eckhart: A Modern Translation* [New York: Harper Torchbooks, 1941], 236, #9)

TO KNOW HOW TO USE SILENCE IS TO KNOW HOW TO MAKE USE OF TIME

The philosopher Blaise Pascal used to say that all human unhappiness is caused by one single thing: our not knowing how to keep still in one place. But quiet is not the only virtue that is out of fashion today. We ourselves have become "time invalids," so to speak. We seem to need to live seven lives in a single day, breathless, stressed, distracted, and half asleep. A peaceful passing of time is not enough for us. From the extended hours of our working day to the need to be almost continually in touch with people, we enter into a smothering cycle of attention, activity, and consumption/exhaustion. "Hurry! Hurry!" is the order issued by a voice that keeps us prisoner and whose face we do not see. "Hurry for what?" There are times when, if we had to explain the deep reasons for our whirlwind activity, we would not be able to do so. And from this too, this failure to reply, we prefer to flee.

Who is it that robs us of time? An American social investigator, Alec Mackenzie, amused himself by creating a list of "thieves of time" and concluded that the most dangerous of these are the interior ones, the ones that we harbor within ourselves. Clearly, there are a great many "extraneous thieves": the casual way we interrupt one another with trivialities; ceaseless long telephone calls for no special reason; social commitments and duties that are to a large extent unnecessary; meetings without a properly prepared agenda. But the most devastating "thieves" are the interior ones, when our own priorities seem to be confused and fluctuating; when we are unable to prepare a daily or monthly plan and be faithful to it; when our responsibilities are badly organized and we refuse to delegate; when we are unable simply to say "No"; when we allow ourselves to become involved in an avalanche of activism and chaos, or when the opposite problem imprisons us: an idealized perfectionism that leaves us paralyzed.

Acquiring a human rhythm for life is not something that comes about all at once, nor can it be achieved in penny-pinching doses. Here too we are faced with a road to transformation that each one must travel and that requires of us truth, apprenticeship, and renunciation. The first renunciation is to relinquish our obsession with being all-powerful. We must have the courage to perceive and accept our limitations, ask for help more often, say "enough for today," without a nagging feeling of guilt. The feeling of insecurity caused by the speed with which everything happens makes us afraid to turn out the light or tidy up the papers in order to continue tomorrow. On the other hand, we need to learn how to plan our day-by-day schedule with wisdom, arranging our activities in order of importance, and better concentrating our energies. We need to learn how to rationalize and to simplify, above all in the case of those tasks that can be foreseen or that are repetitive. And in this way to gain time in order to rediscover those simple pleasures to which only slowness and silence will give us access. How lovely are certain moments of recollection and rest in which our gaze or our footsteps wander aimlessly, in a gratuitousness that, though only a spark, lights up again.

FRIENDS ARE MASTERS OF SILENCE

Silence is an instrument of friendship. The composer John Cage probed the possibility of a work without sound, but was prevented by two things: doubt whether such a task would not prove to be destined to failure from the beginning because everything is sound; and the conviction that such a composition would be incomprehensible in the mental space of Western culture. However, he was encouraged by the experiments that were taking place in the visual arts, particularly by the work of a close friend, the painter Robert Rauschenberg. Above all, Rauschenberg's paintings in the white-on-white series fascinated him. Thus, in 1952, he performed his piece 4'33" for the first time. John Cage's idea, interpreted at the instrument on that occasion by David Tudor, was completely unusual: the musicians were to appear on the stage, greet the audience, sit down at the instrument, and remain there, in silence, for four minutes and thirty-three seconds, after which they were to stand up once again, thank the audience, and leave the stage. The audience expressed its disapproval and there was a storm of boos and hisses. But to the end of his life, John Cage spoke of this piece with deep reverence: "My most important piece is this silent one; no day goes by without my making use of that piece in my life and in my work. I always think of it before I write the next piece."

21

WE BID ONE ANOTHER
FAREWELL MANY TIMES

Saying farewell is perhaps the most difficult aspect of friendship. There is not much one can say. I think we learn slowly, sometimes at great cost, sometimes more serenely, but both are part of the process. I learned something about the art of saying goodbye with the Italian poet Tonino Guerra and his wife. It is a Russian tradition (or at least that is how they accounted for it). Before bidding one another farewell, we met together for a few minutes in complete silence. And then we said goodbye to one another quite lightly, almost happily, as if we were not really parting from one another. Those moments of silence, however, had bound our hearts together much more closely than a few words could have done. When, in the many partings in life, we feel, inevitably, that something or indeed everything has been left unsaid, it is good to recall what the period of silence had said from heart to heart. It may well be that there is no better language in the world for the things we are capable of sharing than silence.

Even when we think that we have not said goodbye, the truth is that, deep down, we say goodbye many times. And this is marvelous. Life has given us this. To have seen one another depart and return, to say goodbye and hello with the certainty that there has been no break, to hear again a thousand times the voices of those we love, thereby prolonging the extraordinary, the unending encounter.

THE PAIN OF SEPARATION

The pain of separation is greater than any word, but words hold onto us as it were while certain departures slowly make their emptiness felt. They are the fragile handrail that supports us when the earth seems to be giving way beneath our feet.

One of the loveliest elegies of friendship, in which the entire drama of loss is spelled out, is the one addressed by David, king and poet, to his friend Jonathan (2 Sam 1:19–20; 25–26):

> Your glory, O Israel, lies slain upon your high places!
>   How the mighty have fallen!
> Tell it not in Gath,
>   proclaim it not in the streets of Ashkelon;
> or the daughters of the Philistines will rejoice,
>   the daughters of the uncircumcised will exult.
>
> How the mighty have fallen
>   in the midst of the battle!
>
> Jonathan lies slain upon your high places.
>   I am distressed for you, my brother Jonathan.

The tears of Jesus by the tomb of his dead friend also speak of the pain of separation:

> When Mary came where Jesus was and saw him, she knelt at his feet and said to him, "Lord, if you had been here, my brother would not have died." When Jesus saw her weeping, and the Jews who came with her also weeping, he was greatly disturbed in spirit and deeply moved. He said, "Where have you laid him?" They said to him, "Lord, come

and see." Jesus began to weep. So the Jews said, "See how he loved him!" (John 11:32–36)

St. Gregory Nazianzen and St. Basil were born in the same year, AD 330. They first met as teenagers in Caesarea of Cappadocia, but it was as fellow students in Athens that they became close friends. "Like streams of a river, from the same source in our native land…so were Basil and I," Gregory was to write later, as he recalled those years. Temperamentally, they were very different. Basil had a very strong, energetic personality whereas Gregory was more of a poet, more given to contemplation. But, even at times of great tension between them, their mutual affection remained intact. Basil died in January 379, at the early age of 49. It fell to St. Gregory to preach the homily during the funeral Mass. It is an unforgettable tribute to friendship: "Sharing the same lodging, the same table, the same sentiments, our eyes fixed on the one goal, as our mutual affection grew ever warmer and stronger. If there was any contest between us, it was not as to who should have the first place for himself, but how he could yield to the other. For each of us regarded the achievement of the other as his own. We seemed to have a single soul animating two bodies."

FRIENDS MAKE US HEIRS

Some friends make us heirs of a place, others of a dwelling, others of a reason for living. Some friends leave us the map after a journey, or the boat in some bay, still hidden in the undergrowth, or the wide-open and irresistible blue that prompted their request. There are friends who initiate us into deciphering the fire, listening to the silences of the earth, into understanding ourselves. There are friends who lead us to the middle of the woods, to the geography of cities, to the secret that lights up the semi-darkness in the temple, to the goodness of God.

Through our friends, we discover the vastness of an inner world, intact and moving like an underlying landscape at the bottom of the sea and, for this very reason, both primordial and delicate, hidden and sublime. We receive help from our friends when we are at a loss for words (or something else we are not sure about, which may not be words) to describe in ourselves the height of our joy or depth of our sorrow. A look from them is a gift given to life; it is breath, pure energy; and it has for us an inexhaustible power of recovery.

Our friends endure with us, and by our side, the hard and the light-as-a-feather mystery of existence. Even when the days grow pale or break into splinters, friendship has the capacity to put back together, from rock bottom, the pieces that have broken off or have been scattered, the unspeakable opposites of the soul: night and day, sorrow and laughter, action and contemplation, life and death.

It may well be that the most fruitful question to ask when our friends die is not so much: "Why have they gone?" What it will take us the rest of our lives to answer, always in complete gratitude, is rather "Why did they come?"

BIBLIOGRAPHY

Aelred of Rievaulx. *Spiritual Friendship*. Edited by Marsha L. Dutton. Translated by Lawrence C. Braceland. Collegeville, MN: Cistercian Publications, 2010.

Agamben, Giorgio. "L'amico." In *What Is An Apparatus: And Other Essays*, translated by David Kishik and Stefan Pedatella. Stanford, CA: Stanford University Press, 2009.

Aristotle. *Nicomachean Ethics*. New York: Cambridge University Press, 2000.

Augustine of Hippo. *Confessions*.

Auster, Paul. *The Invention of Solitude*. New York: Penguin, 1982.

Baldini, Massimo. *L'amicizia secondo i Santi e i Mistici*. Brescia: Queriniana, 1998.

Barthes, Roland. *Mythologies*. New York: Hill and Wang, 2012.

Basset, Lytta. *La Joie Imprenable*. Geneva: Labor et Fides, 1996.

Bernard, Charles André. *Théologie Affective*. Paris: Cerf, 1984.

Bidart, Claire. *L'Amitié, un Lien Social*. Paris: La Découverte, 1997.

Blanchot, Maurice. *L'Amitié*. Paris: Gallimard, 1971.

Bloom, Allan David. *Love and Friendship*. New York: Simon & Schuster, 2000.

Bonhoeffer, Dietrich. *Résistance et Soumission*. Geneva: Labor et Fides, 1963.

Buber, Martin. *I and Thou*. New York: Scribner Classics, 2000.

Calvo, José Maria Zamora, ed. *La Amistad en la Filosofía Antigua*. Madrid: Universidad Autónoma de Madrid, 2009.

Carmichael, Liz. *Friendship: Interpreting Christian Love*. London: T. & T. Clark, 2006.

Cicero. *De Amicitia*. In *On Living and Dying Well*. Translated by Thomas N. Habinek. New York: Penguin, 2012.

Comte, Robert, et al. *L'Avventura dell'amicizia*. Magnano, Italy: Edizioni Qiqajon, 2007.

Coste, René. *L'Amitié avec Jésus*. Paris: Cerf, 2012.

de Certeau, Michel. *La Faiblesse de Croire*. Paris: Seuil, 1987.

Derrida, Jacques. *The Politics of Friendship*. New York: Verso, 1997.

Dolto, Françoise. *Solitude*. Paris: Gallimard, 1994.

Dimitri el Murr, ed. *L'amitié*. Paris: Flammarion, 2001.

Feuillet, André. *Le Mystère de l'Amour Divin dans la Théologie Johannique*. Paris: Gabalda, 1972.

Fitzgerald, John T., ed. *Friendship, Flattery and Frankness of Speech: Studies on Friendship in the New Testament World*. Leiden, NY: E. J. Brill, 1996.

Francis de Sales. *Introduction to the Devout Life*. Brewster, MA: Paraclete Press, 2013.

Garzonio, Marco. *Lazzaro: L'Amicizia nella Bibbia*. Milan: Paoline, 1994.

Godelier, Maurice. *The Enigma of the Gift*. Chicago: University of Chicago Press, 1999.

Gregory Nazianzen. "Funeral Oration for Basil the Great." In *Funeral Orations*. Translated by Leo P. McCauley. Washington, DC: Catholic University of America Press, 2004.

Gruen, Arno. *The Betrayal of the Self: The Fear of Autonomy in Men and Women*. New York: Grove Press, 1988.

Gueullette, Jean-Marie. "*L'amitié dans la communauté: les enjeux théologiques d'une histoire complexe.*" *Revue des sciences philosophiques et théologiques* 2 (2003): 199–219.

———. *L'Amitié, une Épiphanie*. Paris: Cerf, 2004.

Légasse, Simon. "*L'étendue de l'amour interhumain d'après le Nouveau Testament: limites et promesses.*" *Revue théologique de Louvain* 8 (1977): 137–59, 293–304.

Lévi-Strauss, Claude. *The Raw and the Cooked*. Chicago: University of Chicago Press, 1996.

Lispector, Clarice. *Discovering the World*. Manchester: Carcanet, 1992.

Llull, Ramon. *The Book of the Lover and the Beloved*. New York: Paulist Press, 1995.

Marconcini, Benito. *Gli Amici di Dio. Nelle più Belle Pagine della Bibbia*. Milan: Paoline, 2007.

Maritain, Raïssa. *We Have Been Friends Together* and *Adventures in Grace*. Garden City, NY: Image, 1961.

Montaigne, Michel de. *On Friendship*. New York: Penguin Books, 2005.

Nietzsche, Friedrich. *The Gay Science*. New York: Vintage Books, 1974.

Pasquetto, Virgilio. *Il "Volto amico" di Dio disegnato dalla Bibbia*. Vatican City: Libreria Editrice Vaticana, 2010.

Plato. *The Symposium*. Translated by Christopher Gill. London: Penguin, 2003.

Radcliffe, Timothy. *I Call You Friends*. London, New York: Continuum, 2001.

Ricci, Matteo. *On Friendship: One Hundred Maxims for a Chinese Prince*. New York: Columbia University Press, 2009.

Ronchi, Ermes. *Os Beijos não dados. Tu és Beleza*. Prior Velho, Paulinas, 2012.

Seneca. *Ad Lucilium*. Translated by Richard Mott Gummere. http://en.wikisource.org/wiki/Moral_letters_to_Lucilius. Accessed March 13, 2014.

Steiner, George. *Fragments (un peu roussis)*. Paris: Pierre-Guillaume de Roux, 2012.

Weil, Simone. *Waiting for God*. New York: Harper Perennial, 2009.

Wilde, Oscar. "The Devoted Friend." In *The Happy Prince and Other Tales*. London: D. Nutt, 1910.